BUILDING
NUMBER
SENSE THROUGH THE
COMMON CORE

BUILDING
NUMBER
SENSE THROUGH THE
COMMON CORE

Bradley S. Witzel ▪ Paul J. Riccomini ▪ Marla L. Herlong

CORWIN
A SAGE Company

CORWIN
A SAGE Company

FOR INFORMATION:

Corwin

A SAGE Company

2455 Teller Road

Thousand Oaks, California 91320

(800) 233-9936

www.corwin.com

SAGE Publications Ltd.

1 Oliver's Yard

55 City Road

London EC1Y 1SP

United Kingdom

SAGE Publications India Pvt. Ltd.

B 1/I 1 Mohan Cooperative Industrial Area

Mathura Road, New Delhi 110 044

India

SAGE Publications Asia-Pacific Pte. Ltd.

3 Church Street

#10-04 Samsung Hub

Singapore 049483

Printed in the United States of America.

A catalog record of this book is available from the Library of Congress.

ISBN 978-1-4522-0255-6

This book is printed on acid-free paper.

Acquisitions Editor: Jessica Allan

Editorial Assistant: Lisa Whitney

Production Editor: Cassandra Margaret Seibel

Copy Editor: Melinda Masson

Typesetter: C&M Digitals (P) Ltd.

Proofreader: Rae-Ann Goodwin

Indexer: Virgil Diodato

Cover Designer: Janet Kiesel

Permissions Editor: Karen Ehrmann

SUSTAINABLE FORESTRY INITIATIVE

Certified Chain of Custody
Promoting Sustainable Forestry
www.sfiprogram.org
SFI-01268

SFI label applies to text stock

12 13 14 15 16 10 9 8 7 6 5 4 3 2 1

Contents

Acknowledgments

Building number sense in young children isn't easy, especially considering the challenges that schools are facing. We wish to thank the many educators and children who taught us so much about teaching from the common core. This book would not be possible without their collaboration, coaching, and advice.

Publisher's Acknowledgments

Corwin gratefully acknowledges the contributions of the following reviewers:

David Bateman
Professor of Special Education
Shippensburg University
Shippensburg, PA

Susan Birnie
Curriculum Developer
Alexandria City Public Schools
Alexandria, VA

Deborah Gordon
Third Grade Teacher
Madison School District
Phoenix, AZ

Annmarie Urso
Assistant Professor
Ella Cline Shear School of Education
State University of New York at Geneseo
Geneseo, NY

About the Authors

Bradley S. Witzel, PhD, is an award-winning teacher and professor who works as an associate professor and education program coordinator at Winthrop University, the flagship education college for the state of South Carolina. As a classroom teacher, and before that as a paraeducator, he worked in multiple settings teaching mainly math and science to high-achieving students with disabilities. Dr. Witzel has written five books, including the best-selling *Response to Intervention in Math* through Corwin, as well as several dozen book chapters, research and practitioner articles, and training manuals. He has also produced six education videos and several hundred conference and workshop presentations. He is a selected member of the Governing Board of the Southeast Regional Educational Laboratory (REL), funded by the Institute of Education Sciences (IES), and of the Smarter Balanced Assessment Consortium (SBAC) Accessibility and Accommodations work group. Dr. Witzel currently serves as the editor of *Focus on Inclusive Education* through the Association for Childhood Education International (ACEI) and recently served as a panelist on the IES practice guide *Assisting Students Struggling with Mathematics* and as an invited reviewer of the final report from the National Mathematics Advisory Panel. Most importantly, he is a father of two, husband of an educator, and son of two educators.

Paul J. Riccomini is an experienced classroom teacher, author, mathematician, and leading special education expert. Dr. Riccomini began his career as a dual-certified general education mathematics teacher of students with learning disabilities, emotional and behavioral disabilities, and gifted and talented students in Grades 7–12. He taught mathematics to both general and special education students in inclusive settings. He is coauthor of the best-selling *Response to Intervention in Math* (Corwin, 2009) book and is an associate professor of education at the Pennsylvania State University. His teaching experiences required him to have both strong content knowledge in mathematics and to develop and maintain strong collaborative relationships with both general and special educators. As a former middle and high school mathematics teacher, he knows firsthand the challenges faced by students who struggle in mathematics and recognizes the importance of early mathematics development. He hopes the writing of this book will assist teachers in their efforts to develop young mathematicians.

Dr. Riccomini provides professional development in schools across the nation. His dynamic presentations offer research-validated practices that focus on the development of improved instructional practices for all students. Dr. Riccomini's written work includes numerous research and practitioner articles for students with and without learning disabilities, including one of the first books to address Response to Intervention in the area of mathematics. Additional publications he coauthored include three Tier 2 Interventions for the areas of fractions, integers, and simple equations.

 **Marla Larson Herlong**, MEd, earned her bachelor of science in early childhood and her master of education in curriculum and instruction with a concentration in mathematics at Winthrop University in South Carolina. An experienced classroom teacher, she has taught a wide variety of students from kindergarten through second grade. A popular speaker, she has presented several workshops and conference sessions in the areas of math intervention strategies, integrating content, teaching math through problem solving, data-driven assessments, and increasing student engagement. She is currently working on deconstructing assessments and aligning curriculum maps for the Common Core State Standards. Marla was born and raised in California and currently resides in Aiken, South Carolina, with her husband and daughter.

1

Introduction to the Characteristics of Number Sense

To achieve in mathematics, students must acquire a good sense of numbers early in their academic career.

Bradley S. Witzel

Introduction

A young boy and his father visit the beach for the first time. They leave their hotel, lay down their towels in the sand, and then run to the water. Immediately, they fall in love with the waves. They splash wildly among them, riding the surf into shore and then running out as far as the waves crest. They do this back and forth for about an hour. After exhaustion, they decide to check back to where they laid down their towels. However, when they turn to the shore, nothing looks the same. In fact, the high-rise hotel is nowhere in sight. Nervous, they wonder how they got there and, more importantly, how to get back to wherever they started. What had seemed like such a fun, new, and exciting time had taken them to an area where they didn't want to be.

When math education leaders made it a priority to make math more meaningful, the excellent idea was to focus more instruction on the purpose and meaning of mathematical principles rather than memorization and practice. At first, teachers created a balance between the why and the how of mathematics. However, after some years, a few argued that the why of mathematics is more important than the how. Many listened, and changes began. Modeling was de-emphasized, accuracy was devalued, and practice was limited. To some extent, these changes worked. Student engagement increased, math class was more inviting and exciting, and, as a result, students enjoyed math more than ever before. However, students' mathematics performance was not maintained.

Over the past few decades, students in the United States, especially those who show difficulties early, have underwhelmed on international mathematics achievement assessments. Statistics from international assessments and reports suggest students from the United States lack the skills to compete in an international arena, especially in fields requiring proficiency in mathematics (National Center for Education Statistics, n.d.; National Mathematics Advisory Panel [NMAP], 2008). In the example above, the great idea of playing in the waves was fun, but the father and son lost their focus. What has been learned about student engagement and activity cannot be lost, but rigor cannot be sacrificed. We have to keep our vision on learning and achievement for all students, even—and maybe especially—those who struggle early.

Turning Around Math Achievement

Within the United States, proficiency in mathematics has grown as a concern among educators, parents, policy makers, and researchers. Success in mathematics is linked to graduation, higher education, and employment (NMAP, 2008). Over the past decade, many experts have collaborated in efforts such as the Mathematics Learning Study Committee (Kilpatrick, Swafford, & Findell, 2001) and the National Mathematics Advisory Panel (NMAP, 2008) to address educational issues pertaining to mathematics proficiency. A growing consensus among experts indicates many students require curricula that provide a better foundation in mathematical number sense and more effective instruction that is grounded in research (e.g., NMAP, 2008). In order to reach goals such as increased student graduation, competitive access to higher education, and gainful employment, the NMAP emphasized the need for student success in algebra. The NMAP, therefore, recommends that students develop aptitude in prerequisite skills to algebra prior to entering high school. For this reason, particular attention must be paid to the acquisition of the concepts and skills that together develop a student's number sense.

As a result of the overall lackluster mathematical performance, prominent federally supported documents, renewed instructional emphasis of mathematics, and a significant increase in student and school expectations, educators across the United States are changing instruction to improve the mathematics learning of students. Within this discussion, several initiatives have come to the forefront, according to Riccomini and Smith (2011):

- Emphasizing number sense at all levels, but especially in the early grade levels
- Stressing the importance of high-quality mathematics instruction for all students
- Creation and adoption of the Common Core State Standards
- Setting up before- and after-school opportunities for additional mathematics instruction for struggling students
- Renewed effort to raise the awareness of importance of parents' involvement in their child's mathematics education
- Increasing the opportunities for high-quality professional development focused on evidence-based instructional techniques and strategies in the area of mathematics

Adding to the focused efforts above, a considerable paradigm shift has taken place regarding the mechanisms and procedures to address the academic needs of students who have traditionally struggled. Initially focused on early literacy, response to intervention (RTI) has quickly expanded to mathematics (Riccomini & Smith, 2011; Riccomini & Witzel, 2010). One might call the collective attention to mathematics the "perfect instructional storm" because no one at any level, from parents to interventionists, is immune to the concerns and changes within the U.S. education system.

**Textbox 1.1   Math Takes a Back Seat to Reading
Even at Birth**

I recently celebrated the birth of my third child. The morning that we were leaving the hospital, we were given a rather large set of material. Even though I am not a new father, I decided to thumb through the massive

(Continued)

(Continued)

packet of information given to new mothers in my state—maybe all mothers in the United States. As I looked through the documents, I came to several brochures outlining the importance of parents helping their newborn begin to develop important literacy skills. I thought that was fantastic and quickly turned to the next set of documents hoping to see a similar set of brochures focused on parents helping their newborn child learn important early numeracy skills. Much to my dismay, but not to my surprise, there was no such brochure. As a matter of fact, the entire document was void of any information related to "things" parents could do to help foster important pieces of early number sense. I guess this is probably one of the biggest differences compared to other countries—that mathematics takes a back seat to most everything else in the United States.

To make a change in education, it is important to start at the beginning. This book focuses on the construct of mathematical number sense. In this chapter, we discuss the definitions of number sense and the more prevalent core elements within and across the definitions. We conclude with number sense as outlined in the Common Core State Standards (CCSS).

Number Sense Defined

The term *number sense* means different things to different people. In a recent meeting, teachers revealed several perceived definitions of number sense covering anything from numeral recognition to conceptual understandings of complex problem solving. In order to explore instructional aspects of teaching number sense, everyone must agree on the definition. It is important to note that number sense is not necessarily a new construct in mathematics, but rather one that is only recently receiving a great deal of attention. With this renewed attention, many educators and researchers are looking for better and more expansive descriptions. Regardless of the source and definition, common elements emerge across definitions.

Holistically, Gersten and Chard (1999) described number sense as follows:

> Number sense is an emerging construct (Berch, 1998) that refers to a child's fluidity and flexibility with numbers, the sense of what numbers mean and an ability to perform mental mathematics and to look at the world and make comparisons. (p. 18)

To operationalize number sense, the NMAP (2008) provided the following description:

> In its most fundamental form, number sense entails an ability to immediately identify the numerical value associated with small quantities; . . .
>
> - [T]his more highly developed form of number sense should extend to numbers written in fraction, decimal, and exponential forms. . . .
> - [P]oor number sense interferes with learning algorithms and number facts and prevents use of strategies to verify if solutions to problems are reasonable. (p. 27)

Geary, Hoard, and Hamson (1999) attempted to explore more specific details of number sense and reported that students with disabilities begin to demonstrate difficulties with counting knowledge, number naming and writing, and retrieval of facts as early as first grade when compared to students without disabilities. Suggesting that these early misconceptions and difficulties in the foundational pieces of basic mathematics will likely affect students' future mathematical outcomes, they labeled these problems as important pieces of number sense. The suggestion by Gersten and Chard (1999) was later confirmed by researchers who examined growth trajectories of kindergarten students with disabilities (Morgan, Farkas, & Wu, 2009). They concluded that 70% of students in the lowest 10th percentile at the start and finish of kindergarten were likely to remain in the same percentile five years later. Clearly, students who fail to acquire the pieces that make up number sense as early as kindergarten are at greatest risk for failure in mathematics in the long term.

Textbox 1.2   A Checklist of a Numerically Powerful Child

1. Develops *meaning* for numbers and operations.

   Developing meaning of numbers and operations related to real life contexts is crucial for the subsequent three categories. Since children are exposed to meaning of numbers very early through daily living activities, it is important for formal mathematics instruction to continue to develop quantity, associations between and within the four operations as well as recognizing and generating differing representations of numbers. This category forms the foundation of future number sense development.

(Continued)

(Continued)

2. Looks for *relationships* among numbers and operations.

   In this category, formal knowledge of numbers and operations begins to take shape by extending the meaning developed initially. Students are able to decompose numbers in varying forms ($2 + 6 = 8$; $2 + 4 + 2 = 8$; $8 - 6 = 2$) and begin to recognize how numbers and operations are interconnected. The interconnectedness of mathematics is essential for the correct application of strategies and procedures.

3. *Understands* computation strategies and uses them appropriately and efficiently.

   In this category, students begin to apply formal rules and procedures with an understanding of why a specific procedure or algorithm is appropriate. Students pay more attention to accuracy and precision in their answers as well as demonstrating flexibility with various strategies based on the context of the problem. Estimation becomes a crucial piece in the development of the understanding of efficient and correct strategies.

4. *Makes sense* of numerical and quantitative situations.

   In this category, students begin to develop and seek out calculations and relationships that make sense in the context of real life problems. The "making sense" of mathematics in this category is based on the execution of strategies and algorithms resulting in precise answers that are context dependent. Students' development with the ability to make sense of answers in the real world is the cornerstone of the application of mathematics, the ultimate goal of mathematics teaching.

Source: Adapted from Charles & Lobato (2000).

The Common Core State Standards

While every state has enacted new policies to improve mathematics education, almost every state has adopted a common list of standards intended to drive instruction for years to come. The Common Core State Standards (CCSS) were recently created as a set of sequential grade-level expectations meant to replace individual state standards. Many of the states and schools that have already begun teaching the CCSS report that expectations are more rigorous with clearer progressions across grade levels. Proponents of these new benchmarks see them as a means of improving the academic achievement of U.S. students. Those who live in states that have not fully adopted the CCSS should still expect an impact from these standards because of changes in textbook content to satisfy the majority of states that have adopted the standards. For more information on the CCSS, see www.corestandards.org.

Despite the large number of states involved and the number of people affected by this shift in standards and increased expectations, many are still concerned about the CCSS. Will state assessments be validated in time? How will current instructional materials be adapted to implement the CCSS? Who is helping prepare administrators, instructional coaches, teachers, interventionists, and parents for the changes? Many questions need to be answered during this process of change. Many educators may view these changes as merely another passing fad, theoretical model, or "best practice." Instead, these changes represent a substantive alteration in curricula and instructional emphasis. The CCSS will likely result in increased instructional rigor and a more focused approach to number sense.

The CCSS and Elements of Number Sense

Students must be taught differently than before, at least for younger grade levels. For example, one notable change from the CCSS splits the previously developed NCTM operations standard into (a) operations and algebraic thinking and (b) operations and the base-10 language. Operations designed to lead to algebraic facility allow children to learn the relationship between addition and subtraction using notation other than whole numbers (e.g., $7 + n = 15; 15 - n = 7$). The operations and base-10 standard strand focus on operational facility based on place value that reinforces the presentation of numbers as multiples of 10. These examples are only part of the changes suggested by the CCSS that underlie the increased emphasis on number sense.

Of the 22 kindergarten common core standards, 14 can be directly linked to elements of number sense. Shown in Table 1.1 is a trajectory of the number sense elements included in the CCSS across Grades K–3. Counting and numeral and number recognition begin early, and proficiency is expected by the end of Grade 1. Magnitude comparisons with single-digit comparisons begin in

Table 1.1   Trajectory of Number Sense Elements Included in the CCSS Across Grades K–3

Number Sense Component	Kindergarten Common Core Standard	First-Grade Common Core Standard	Second-Grade Common Core Standard	Third-Grade Common Core Standard
Numeral and Number Recognition				
Magnitude Comparisons (place value)				
Counting Principles			Begins with fractions	
Fact Fluency				
Math Language				

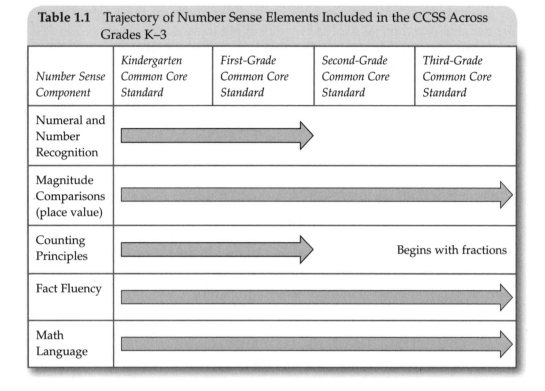

kindergarten, but understanding and applying place value begin soon afterward and continue as part of solving operations. Different from years past, fact fluency is emphasized early and often. From addition and subtraction to multiplication and division, math language is implied throughout the grades. However, even in kindergarten, problem solving begins in a concrete manner. By first grade, word problems begin using addition.

Book Content

The elements of number sense that we emphasize in this book include quantity and cardinality (Chapter 4), numeral and number recognition (Chapter 4), strategic counting (Chapter 4), magnitude comparisons (Chapters 4 and 5), fact fluency (Chapters 4 through 6), multiplication and division (Chapter 6), algebraic concepts (Chapter 7), math language and problem solving (Chapter 8), and vocabulary (Chapter 9). In addition, we address mastery learning (Chapter 2), assessment within number sense (Chapter 3), and how to combine literacy in math and integrate math across course content (Chapter 10).

References

Berch, D. B. (1998, April). *Mathematical cognition: From numerical thinking to mathematics education.* Paper presented at the National Institute of Child Health and Human Development, Bethesda, MD.

Charles, R., & Lobato, J. (2000). *Future basics: Developing numerical power.* Denver, CO: National Council of Supervisors of Mathematics.

Common Core State Standards for Mathematics. (n.d.). Retrieved June 1, 2011, from the Council of Chief State School Officers and National Governor's Association website: http://corestandards.org/assets/CCSSI_Math%20 Standards.pdf

Geary, D. C., Hoard, M. K., & Hamson, C. O. (1999). Numerical and arithmetical cognition: Patterns of functions and deficits in children at risk for a mathematical disability. *Journal of Experimental Child Psychology, 74*(3), 213–239.

Gersten, R., & Chard, D. (1999). Number sense: Rethinking arithmetic instruction for students with mathematical disabilities. *Journal of Special Education, 33*(1), 18–28.

Gersten, R., Clarke, B., Haymond, K., & Jordan, N. (2011). *Screening for mathematics difficulties in K–3 students* (2nd ed.). Portsmouth, NH: RMC Research Corporation, Center on Instruction.

Kilpatrick, J., Swafford, J., & Findell, B. (Eds.). (2001). Conclusions and recommendations. In *Adding it up: Helping children learn mathematics* (pp. 407–432). Washington, DC: Mathematics Learning Study Committee, Center for Education, Division of Behavioral and Social Sciences and Education, National Research Council, National Academies Press.

Morgan, P. L., Farkas, G., & Wu, Q. (2009). Kindergarten predictors of recurring externalizing and internalizing psychopathology in 3rd and 5th grade. *Journal of Emotional and Behavioral Disorders, 17,* 67–79.

National Center for Education Statistics. (n.d.). *Trends in International Mathematics and Science Study (TIMSS): TIMSS 2007 results.* Retrieved May 26, 2012, from http://nces.ed.gov/timss/results07.asp

National Mathematics Advisory Panel. (2008). *Foundations for success: The final report of the National Mathematics Advisory Panel.* Washington DC: U.S. Department of Education.

Riccomini, P. J., & Smith, G. W. (2011). Introduction of response to intervention in mathematics. In R. Gersten & R. Newman-Gonchar (Eds.), *Response to intervention in mathematics* (pp. 1–16). Baltimore: Brookes.

Riccomini, P. J., & Witzel, B. S. (2010). *Response to intervention in math.* Thousand Oaks, CA: Corwin.

2

Redefining Mastery Through Long-Term Planning

Working with young children is one of the more personally rewarding careers one can have. The work can be exhilarating and inspiring, and capturing the entirety of a young person's energy is a challenge. Great planning must go into using children's enthusiasm to build the foundation for mathematical excellence.

How to Prepare Children for Mathematics Understanding

Mathematics understanding is a holistic idea that entails people using multiple facets of mathematics to work through problems and reason logically. To accomplish such understanding, particularly at higher levels of mathematics, it is important to be practiced with multiple math skills and know how to use them collectively. As discussed in Chapter 1, this understanding is looked at as number sense. Thus, although we attempt to break down early mathematics understanding into a set of skills, the interrelationship of these skills is inseparable. With the increase of one skill, another skill follows. For example, as a student understands a mental number line more accurately, magnitude comparisons should become easier, as should place value. Likewise, as a student grows in her understanding of place value, so should her ability to complete magnitude comparisons. Once magnitude comparisons are more readily understood, subtraction may be more aptly comprehended.

Building mathematics skills from one to the next must be consciously planned and taught appropriately. The goal is for long-term success rather than simply short-term gain alone. However, it is important not to mistake the development of mathematical skills as those often mentioned in discussion of developmentally appropriate practice (DAP). DAP should be viewed as building from precursor skills in a vertical fashion rather than waiting for skills to be possible based on age level. The National Mathematics Advisory Panel (NMAP, 2008) clearly stated,

> Claims based on Piaget's highly influential theory, and related theories of "developmental appropriateness" that children of particular ages cannot learn certain content because they are "too young," "not in the appropriate stage," or "not ready" have consistently been shown to be wrong. Nor are claims justified that children cannot learn particular ideas because their brains are insufficiently developed, even if they possess the prerequisite knowledge for learning the ideas. (p. 30)

Thus, when focusing on the application of DAP in mathematics, it is important to view the progressions of learning rather than age-level limitations.

Just as one math skill builds on and with another, so too do the methods by which a student learns. As Wu (1999) stated, there exists a false dichotomy of whether students learn first through conceptual understanding or through procedures. The truth is that accurate and efficient procedural understanding, not simple regurgitation, builds conceptual understanding. Likewise, to understand a concept cannot happen without procedural comprehension. *True mastery is to recognize the problem, understand a solution path, accurately and efficiently fulfill the problem-solving steps to reach the solution, and understand the utility of the process and the reasoning behind the answer.* Therefore, it is best to take former Secretary of Education Richard Riley's advice and forget about math paradigms. Instead, we should focus on what is being taught and how well students are learning the information.

What Is Being Taught

A focus on curriculum is important from the classroom level to a national push for increased rigor. Curriculum here is simply defined as the content that is planned to be taught across grade levels. Organizations like the National Council of Teachers of Mathematics (NCTM), the National Governors Association (NGA), and the Council of Chief State School Officers (CCSSO) have set out independently and, more recently, collectively to develop a curriculum that defines what content should be taught in kindergarten through 12th-grade mathematics and how to organize and task-analyze this content per grade level. From the 1989 Principles and Standards (NCTM) to the more recently accepted Common Core State Standards (CCSS), these suggested standards have set the framework for state departments of education and consequently textbook publishers to develop a scope and sequence of math skills. For many years, states have adopted these principles and dictated standards that every student must achieve per grade level. This standards-based education has been organized by district administration and taught by teachers.

Although standards should dictate a curriculum, not every teacher follows those standards equally. Thus, the curriculum may be different from one class to the next. In one classroom, the curriculum may be a page-by-page sequential presentation of the district- or school-adopted textbook. In another classroom, it may be a collection over several years presented either as math skills or even as a holistic project. Different teachers in the same grade at the same school may even emphasize different algorithms for the same skill. For example, one second-grade teacher may teach subtraction with borrowing while the other teaches subtraction with regrouping using expanded notation. Both present ways of working with place value, but the differences in appearance affect what algorithms a teacher can present first with future math skills, such as multiplication of whole numbers, as is seen in the fourth-grade example as follows. This, in turn, affects how multiples of decimals can be approached.

Second Grade

2.NBT.5. Fluently add and subtract within 100 using strategies based on place value, properties of operations, and/or the relationship between addition and subtraction.

$$6^5 3^{13}$$
$$-1\,8$$
$$\overline{4\,5}$$

$$63 = 60 + 3 = 50 + 13$$
$$-18 = -10 - 8 = -10 - 8$$
$$\overline{40 + 5 = 45}$$

Fourth Grade

4.NBT.5. Multiply a whole number of up to four digits by a one-digit whole number, and multiply two two-digit numbers, using strategies based on place value and the properties of operations. Illustrate and explain the calculation by using equations, rectangular arrays, and/or area models.

$$63$$
$$\times\,18$$
$$\overline{24}$$
$$480$$
$$30$$
$$\underline{600}$$
$$1134$$

×	60	3
10	600	30
8	480	24

$600 + 30 + 480 + 24 = 1134$

Fifth Grade

5.NBT.7. Add, subtract, multiply, and divide decimals to hundredths, using concrete models or drawings and strategies based on place value, properties of operations, and/or the relationship between addition and subtraction; relate the strategy to a written method and explain the reasoning used.

$$6.3$$
$$\times\,1.8$$
$$\overline{.24}$$
$$4.8$$
$$.3$$
$$\underline{+\,6}$$
$$11.34$$

×	6	.3
1	6	.3
.8	4.8	.24

$6 + 0.3 + 4.8 + 0.24 = 11.34$

There are several unintended outcomes from a lack of common curriculum and delivery. If teachers' curriculum is not equivalent, then students in subsequent years will have a myriad of skills, none being equal. This will cause the next teacher to think she is reteaching skills from previous years. In the example above, because the students are used to working from right to left for addition and subtraction in second grade, the fourth-grade teacher can employ a similar strategy with multiplication. However, if the fourth-grade teacher wishes to use an array and begin to use more place value and secondary-style left-to-right approaches, then she will have to reteach place value of each factor. This is an extra step not covered in the standards. Thus, each grade-level team must work in concert to prepare students from one grade to the next. A lack of concerted effort will likely show up on successive grade-level exams.

For accountability, standards-based statewide exams were set in place at specific grade levels to be used as checkpoints to determine how well students are achieving. When a group of students is not achieving to expectations, as indicated on a statewide achievement test, then changes in the curriculum and curriculum delivery leading up to and including that grade level need to be considered. In other words, it is not that grade-level teacher's fault. Likewise, when a group of students is achieving at or above expectations, as indicated on a statewide achievement test, then celebration should go to those delivering curriculum leading up to and including that grade level. In other words, praise should be provided to more than that grade-level teacher. Next, that team needs to talk about continued planning to further increase student achievement. The assessment is merely a checkpoint evaluating the education to that level.

Although not every state has adopted the CCSS, the likelihood that a majority of states will deliver a "potential" national math curriculum should help with curriculum and textbook development, equivalence of education for transient students, and a broader understanding of mathematics rigor necessary for national improvements. "There may be no more challenging educational and theoretical issue than scaling up educational programs across a large number of diverse populations and contexts in the early childhood system in the U.S." (Farran et al., 2011, p. 8). However, unless there develops a more common agreement as to how to teach students and what is expected of students, then there will be difficulty in delivering the CCSS, and thus they will be considered a failure.

In order to develop common agreement on how to teach the required standards, both horizontal and vertical planning are required. Horizontal planning occurs within a grade level or content team in an effort to improve instruction for students in a specific grade or course. Vertical planning occurs across grade levels to improve instruction for students over an extended time period. Both should be based on student outcomes and occur in succession, first with horizontal planning and then with vertical planning.

Horizontal (Grade-Level) Planning

During a second-grade team meeting, four teachers gathered to decide how to improve their students' math learning. The principal asked each teacher to list the most problematic areas of instruction and his or her beliefs about what would improve student learning. What was found was that each teacher listed the same problematic areas of instruction, but each had a different set of beliefs as to what to do. Each teacher listed a different amount of time for math instruction. Two of the teachers wanted the students to learn the newest and most difficult content through discovery learning while the other two believed explicit and systematic instruction was most appropriate. One teacher thought math should be practiced mainly through games while the other three wanted a mix of practice opportunities. The principal realized that each teacher was doing what he or she felt worked rather than what was research-supported. What was needed was an infusion of research.

Most grade-level teams meet biweekly or monthly to discuss problem areas and share lesson ideas. Teams typically discuss student concerns, resources, and lesson ideas. Horizontal planning should be more. This time should be spent helping all team members get on the same page instructionally. This requires discussing grade-level strengths, math areas of concern, establishing nonnegotiables, and research investigations as to how to help. Instructional nonnegotiables should include curriculum consistency, time of instruction, when math instruction should occur, and how to teach some of the more challenging math content.

Analyzing student outcomes reveals grade-level strengths and weaknesses. Based on these data, teams must agree how to improve their instruction specifically to address those weaknesses. For example, many teams find that different teachers use different amounts of time for math instruction. Agreeing on nonnegotiables helps set a baseline from which to start math learning improvements. Table 2.1 is a copy of one team's table used to establish nonnegotiables.

Once a team establishes nonnegotiables, the team needs to meet to decide how to improve specific areas within the mathematics curriculum. When deciding how best to teach a specific skill, it may help to task-analyze instruction by breaking down procedures into smaller

Table 2.1   Example Team Table to Establish Nonnegotiables

Second-grade teacher	Minimal daily time of instruction	Strengths	Concerns	Curriculum
Watkins	60 minutes	Addition and subtraction fluency Test scores	Reasoning	Basal series + computer fluency practice
Richards	45 minutes	Place value within addition and subtraction	Word problems	Basal series
Gonzales	30 minutes	Engagement	Fluency Word problems Test scores	Basal series + math games
Bertram	60 minutes	Engagement Problem solving	Fluency Test scores	Basal series + discovery activities
Team agreed on nonnegotiables				
60 minutes daily	Fluency practice twice per week	Use explicit instruction when introducing new concepts	Discovery activity at the end of each unit	Teach word problem strategies and use at least once daily

steps. Visually comparing two teachers' stepwise approaches will expose their differences in instruction and consequently the differences between what students learn from one class to the next (Riccomini, Witzel, & Riccomini, 2011; Witzel & Riccomini, 2007). In Table 2.2, both teachers listed similar steps to solving the same problem. However, one teacher's think-alouds and steps reveal an emphasis on place value and number magnitude along with mathematics vocabulary.

To determine the best approach to teach the most troublesome components of mathematics, teachers should analyze student outcome data, such as test scores or progress monitoring scores. When team-based action research is not available, teams should seek advice, from either research or another authority, on how to improve student outcomes. Based on the research, grade-level teams must consider integrity and fidelity.

Table 2.2 Visual Comparison of Two Teachers' Stepwise Approaches to Mathematics Instruction

Teacher instructional stepwise comparison of 13 × 6	
Teacher 1	Teacher 2
Write down 13 × 6 vertically. 13 ×6	Write down 13 × 6 vertically. 13 ×6
Multiply 6 and 3 to get 18. Place the 8 ones in the product row under the ones in the factors. Place the 1 ten in the tens column above the top factor. Multiply 6 and 1 ten, and then add the 1 ten written on top to get 7 tens. Write 7 in the tens column in the product area under the problem. The answer is 78.	Multiply 6 and 3 to get 18. Place the 8 in the answer and the 1 over the 1 in 13. Multiply 6 and 1 to get 6 and then add the one you just wrote to get 7. Write 7 to the left of the 8 in the answer. The answer is 78.

Once a team identifies a method and agrees on an approach, team members must be consistent in the implementation. In some cases, it may be necessary to have members sign an agreement form as to how to carry out the method. Next, to help with fidelity, team members should discuss implementation and results and, when possible, visit each other's classes. Involving administration in team-level decisions helps ensure some level of reliability since the method could be included as part of the teacher evaluation process. The concern is that if one or two team members act independently of the agreed-on approach and decide to teach a math skill another way, then students will have mismatched understanding. Such incongruence within a grade level makes it difficult to work as a team to improve student learning. Also, the subsequent grade-level teacher will have a wider range of mathematical understanding, making it more difficult to plan progressions of mathematics.

Keep: "Our grade-level team uses this approach because of its implications for what students learn next year."
Leave: "I teach it this way because that is the way it was taught to me."

Vertical Planning

A young third-grade teacher was honored with an award by his school district primarily because his math scores were among the highest in the state. Upon hearing this, the principal congratulated him and then took him through the school to see what was happening in kindergarten, first-grade, and second-grade mathematics. Humbled by the excellent instruction, he remarked, "I guess I wouldn't have had those scores if the teachers before me hadn't done such an excellent job."

Recently, some policy makers and even school district administrators have argued that teachers should be paid based on their students' test scores. While this may seem logical to some, it is quite difficult and erroneous to conclude that one teacher is superior or inferior to another based on one year's test scores alone. That is because one teacher's class achievements are directly related to the previous teachers' successes and failures. When one teacher makes an error in instruction, that error may compound into other issues that affect students' performance and understanding for grades to come.

According to the National Assessment of Educational Progress (NAEP), in 2007, 15% of fourth-grade students and 25% of eighth-grade students scored below basic in mathematics. In 2011, the NAEP scores revealed that 18% of fourth-grade students and 27% of eighth-grade students scored below basic in mathematics. Not only do too many U.S. students continue to struggle in math, but, once again, increasing numbers of students struggle in successive grade levels. Thus, if a student struggles early in math, those difficulties will be compounded in more difficult mathematics. To counter this trend, it is very important to plan mathematical progressions from one grade to the next.

Following horizontal planning for each grade-level team, representatives from each team should meet to discuss the flow from one grade to the next. In these meetings, it is important to talk about not only student strengths and weaknesses with supportive outcome data, but instructional approaches, allotted time of instruction, and use of materials as well. Specific to the CCSS, there are potential roadblocks that must be planned for appropriately.

Potential Roadblocks

There is potential confusion with the wording of some of the CCSS. In one example, 4.NBT.4 reads "Fluently add and subtract multi-digit whole numbers using the standard algorithm" (CCSS, p. 29) but follows the header "Use place value understanding and properties of operations to perform multi-digit arithmetic" (CCSS, p. 29). Under the same header, 4.NBT.5 reads "Multiply a whole number of up to four digits by a one-digit whole number, and multiply two two-digit numbers, using strategies based on place value and the properties of operations. Illustrate and explain the calculation by using equations, rectangular arrays, and/or area models." In another example, 5.NBT.5 reads "Fluently multiply multi-digit whole numbers using the standard algorithm" (CCSS, p. 35). By "the standard algorithm," some may interpret this to mean the one that each person was already using. After all, that is the standard algorithm. However, "the standard algorithm" means an accurate and efficient algorithm should be used across math skills and grade levels. Be cautious as to the choice of "standard algorithms." Algorithms should be consistent across grade level and mathematical skill as much as possible. To influence the choice of algorithm, other standards, such as 5.NBT.7, state such requirements as "Add, subtract, multiply, and divide decimals to hundredths, using concrete models or drawings and strategies based on place value, properties of operations, and/or the relationship between addition and subtraction; relate the strategy to a written method and explain the reasoning used" (CCSS, p. 35). Thus, if students are to learn strategies based on place value, then the selected algorithm should focus on place value knowledge.

This does not mean that students should only know one algorithm, but rather that they should collectively understand the most efficient one first. Once mastered, students can tackle alternative algorithms. However, introducing more than one way to learn a complex process simultaneously is inefficient and taxes a person's working memory.

One way to plan for this vertical planning is to have a representative from each grade-level team meet together to present his or her group's areas of concern and proposed way of addressing them. Teams will work across grade level to identify patterns of concern and more cohesively decide on their plan of action. Once this plan of action is decided, all grade-level teachers should be held accountable to support the plan with their students.

Once a school sets its vertical planning, then this information should be presented to feeder schools for improved alignment between schools. From these conversations, changes in content emphases will develop to better prepare one grade level for the next so that approaches and strategies are familiar to students (see Table 2.3).

Table 2.3   Vertical Planning for Improved Alignment Between Grade Levels

Grade level	Area of concern	How it will be taught to prepare students for the next grade	Area of concern	How it will be taught to prepare students for the next grade	Area of concern	How it will be taught to prepare students for the next grade
K						
1						
2						
3						
4						

Keep: "What I do this year will directly impact what and how my students do in future years."

Leave: "I want to teach first grade because my math is too weak. That way it won't affect the students on the [statewide exam]."

RTI Framework to Support What Is Being Taught

Horizontal and vertical planning are important but difficult and time consuming. When a school initiates a response-to-intervention (RTI) framework, the time involved in planning increases even more. Reviewing school-wide and grade-level scores on screening and statewide assessments should create overall impressions of student learning of mathematics. Meeting standards on such assessments is necessary but not sufficient for proclaiming mastery of mathematics. However, when too many students are not meeting standards, an emphasis on passing screening and statewide assessments should become the priority. For students in early elementary grades, the focus of interventions should include a heavy emphasis on early numeracy components.

RTI requires not only that Tier 1 teachers organize and coordinate their instruction and intervention but that their work is aligned with Tier 2 and Tier 3 intervention support as well. For example, since Tier 1 instruction planning should include instruction on standard algorithms, then the Tier 2 or 3 interventionist must assess why the algorithm is not understood and how to reteach missing math skills that may be preventing the student from learning. Additionally, interventionists must understand what areas of weakness or concern exist for every grade level. Since difficulty in mathematics appears to increase by grade level, a student who is struggling in higher-level grades will need intervention in more math skills than a student in lower-level grades.

How Math Is Taught

While many might consider how math should be taught to be a controversial topic, it shouldn't be. As long as high-stakes tests exist, how to teach must be based on student outcomes. NMAP (2008) stated that no one approach, teacher-directed or student-directed, is superior, but rather teachers should adjust instruction to the needs of students. When learning is new, difficult, or dangerous, students must be taught explicitly, deliberately, and systematically. Likewise, Clark, Kirschner, and Sweller (2012) concluded that "when teaching new content and skills to novices, teachers are more effective when they provide explicit guidance accompanied by practice and feedback" (p. 6). As students gain mastery of the concept and process, teacher direction fades. Independent student applications work best once students have the skills in order to succeed. Few argue against this sequence when learning to ski or when teaching their children to cross the street because to not teach the skill accurately and to mastery may cause injury or death. Parallel to this, to not provide a sufficient amount of modeling and guided practice before independent student work may cause student failure. In a recent research analysis, Rosenshine (2012) found that "the most successful teacher spent more time in guided practice, more time asking questions, more time checking for understanding, more time correcting errors, and more time having students work out problems with teacher guidance" (p. 16). In the standards for mathematical practices, the CCSS include guidelines on how to teach and what to expect from students. In horizontal and vertical planning meetings, these must be considered.

These practices include the following:

1. Make sense of problems and persevere in solving them.

2. Reason abstractly and quantitatively.

3. Construct viable arguments and critique the reasoning of others.

4. Model with mathematics.

5. Use appropriate tools strategically.

6. Attend to precision.

7. Look for and make use of structure.

8. Look for and express regularity in repeated reasoning.

While redundancy pervades this list, these are key elements that should be included in a mathematics plan for young children. The following extends beyond that in the CCSS for mathematical practice.

1. To make sense of problems, children should be able to solve problems and understand why their approach to a solution makes sense. It is one thing to be able to solve problems through memorization of an algorithm. However, it is much more valuable to know why the algorithm fits the problem set and how to adapt that approach to other problems. For example, when solving a subtraction problem with regrouping, such as 82 – 56, there are several ways to solve the problem. What is important is that the child recognizes the problem type and identifies an approach and then works through the problem in an attempt to solve it. When students are unsuccessful, they require motivation to continue attempts at solving problems.

2. Reasoning needs to be expressed verbally according to the mathematics involved. The reasoning involves verbalization or expression of logic. Most often this reasoning is modeled by another, be it a teacher or a knowledgeable parent. In other occasions, students self-discover mathematical principles. In such cases, the student requires guidance and barriers about possible conclusions when self-reasoning. Efficiency must also be taken into consideration. After all, Newton didn't discover integral calculus in a 90-minute math class. No matter who provides the model of reasoning behind mathematical principles and processes, a clear and accurate model must be present.

3. Students must be able to reason mathematically. Teach math processes and algorithms through reasoning. Help students understand one approach at a time such that once one approach is understood, memorized, and practiced, and then alternative approaches may be introduced. Since most alternative approaches are grounded in the same mathematical reasoning, showing similarities of approaches helps students understand

underlying mathematical principles. For example, a student may first learn subtraction with regrouping through the standard right-to-left algorithm. Once that is mastered, place value may be better understood when solving similar problems using decomposition of numbers using regrouping. Finally, a student may be able to learn the use of a mental number line instead of regrouping when solving similar problems.

$$\begin{array}{r} 42 \\ -14 \\ \hline 28 \end{array}$$

$$\begin{array}{rcl} 42 = & 40 + 2 = & 30 + 12 \\ -14 = & -10 - 4 = & -10 - 4 \\ \hline & & 20 + 8 = 28 \end{array}$$

$$\begin{array}{rcl} 42 & = & 40 + 2 \\ -14 & = & -10 - 4 \\ \hline & & 30 - 2 \end{array}$$

The purpose of using multiple paths to answers is to show similarities in reasoning. For students who tend to not reason well or memorize procedures, it may be necessary to teach students math reasoning by teaching examples from nonexamples to learn which approaches work and why.

4. Students must be able to use math to solve problems. Math modeling consists of applying math in meaningful situations. To prepare mathematical modeling, students must see and hear teachers engage in mathematics problem solving. Think-alouds are a valuable strategy for modeling not only how to solve problems in a stepwise fashion but why certain decisions are made throughout the problem-solving steps. From such think-alouds, students will be able to model problems themselves by explaining their reasoning within math problem solving. Problem solving is a structure—one that may involve complex mathematics and, quite often, no mathematics at all. Problem solving exists well beyond the bounds of mathematics and into the everyday life of students. Helping students recognize the mathematical connections to problem solving helps build relevance to mathematics and shows the interconnectedness of multiple contents. Moreover, students need opportunities to reason mathematically and apply skills in authentic situations to further their mathematics understanding. However, while authentic activities are engaging, they often fail at delivering important skill and conceptual understanding (Wu, 1999). Present authentic problems once students have acquired prerequisite math skills. Also, when providing such authentic situations, it is important to set up

the problems so that students spend time on the mathematics of the problem rather than the reading comprehension challenge found in many word problems. In such cases, teach students how to attack word problems.

5. From concrete manipulatives to peer groupings, many tools can be used to solve problems. There are no absolute winners or losers when it comes to tools. What is important is the use of such tools within strategies to meet the objective. For example, students who have mastered multiplication may use a calculator to expedite their multiplication in a multistep problem. However, giving a student a calculator to help the student go quicker on a multiplication fluency exam does not support that student's learning. The math tool is meant as an instructional instrument and not the instruction itself. For example, Geary (2004) found that some students overly rely on concrete objects, such as fingers, when they are used exclusively and without planned transitions to abstract work.

6. Attention has been tied to better understanding of mathematics (Mann, Moeller, Pixner, Kaufmann, & Nuerk, 2011). Teach students to recognize important parts of mathematics, procedure, reasoning, vocabulary, and principles. For example, when looking at multiple-digit numbers, teach students to look at digit position within the number and connect that digit to value. When subtraction is taught, teach students to recognize whether regrouping and borrowing/stealing are necessary and why.

7. Mathematics learning across many years works in progressions from one topic to the next, building steadily from concept to concept. Students often have a solitary goal when solving a math problem: to get the right answer. However, students must be taught that how they solve a problem has as much to with their success as the answer. This is because how a student solves the problem this year directly impacts his or her approach to solving problems the next year. When math is taught as a series of tricks without reason, then the progression from one math skill to another is lost. To help stress this point, it may be necessary to grade math answers using a multiple-point system where only partial credit is given for the correct answer and the rest of the credit is given for the student's process.

8. Not every math skill requires a new algorithm. When teaching a skill that can be built upon, teach steps that will help students be

successful at the next step. For example, when teaching two-by two-digit multiplication, include steps and reasoning that allow the student to scaffold learning to two by three and three by three as well. If every math skill is as a new math trick, then students will be challenged per their working memory rather than their mathematics ability. Teach efficient approaches to problem solving that work across math skills as often as possible.

Assessment

No longer can educators at any grade level claim student success without assessment results based on student outcomes. In Chapter 3, multiple forms of assessment are addressed from standardized instruments to formative assessment. Assessment informs instruction and curriculum and should be used in decision making for school decisions as well as student placement in RTI models. Use such assessment to determine where and how to teach students. However, interpretation of student outcomes requires caution. Interpreting a student's answers on a screening exam for early number sense should be used *not* to assess ability of mathematical prowess but rather to take a quick look at the student's current level of achievement. This current level may be used to develop a starting place for instruction or intervention. Strengths and weaknesses should be used to determine where and how to intervene. For example, if a student can count and accurately compare single-digit magnitudes but has poor working memory and understanding of place value, then the student needs to be taught place value and will need extra time and possibly alternative instruction with procedural algorithms.

Expectations and Differentiation

> Goal: If we are only helping students learn math as well as we learned it, then our goal is a cycle of mediocrity. To improve mathematics in this country, our goal must be to have students understand it better than we did.

Mathematics rigor must be a focus of everyone involved in mathematics education. Students must master early mathematics foundation skills. When defining mastery, identify the expectation of each lesson based on the verbiage of the standard. Use those standards to differentiate student instruction, increase expectations, and involve parents in the process.

1. Take students from accuracy and reasoning to fluent approaches to automaticity when appropriate. Differentiate expectations based on student and standard. Fade teacher direction as students gain success and mastery. When a new math skill is being introduced, the expectation should be that the student can provide a simple model close to what was presented by the teacher. When a skill appears to be learned, students may solve authentic activities to test the student's application and generalized reasoning.

2. Defining mastery based on short-term successes provides a false sense of accomplishment. It is important to design curriculum reviews every few weeks to challenge students' retention of mathematics. For example, once two skills are learned, a cumulative review should be included to practice past skills. Each successive skill mastered should be included in cumulative reviews.

3. Involve parents throughout the process. Mathematics isn't a 60- or 90-minute-per-day affair. To improve interest, engagement, and generalization, math should be discussed at home, on the playground, and with dolls and plastic soldiers, as well as at school. Math should be performed on paper, verbally, and in structured game situations. With increasing expectations for students, it is necessary to teach parents what is expected in solving problems and even the procedures per skill. Conduct parent workshops and provide written and possibly video directions for parents. Provide homework as maintenance rather than instruction. In other words, make sure that students have documented mastery of a math process before assigning it for homework. This may mean that students are completing homework on different mathematics than was covered that day in class.

The goal of each grade level is not merely to score high on standards-based end-of-grade tests, but rather to prepare students for future coursework in an effort to create mathematically knowledgeable students. This is not an excuse to give up on rigor because subsequent grade levels are not best supporting student learning. Rather, it is a charge to vertically plan better core instruction and curriculum so that one grade level's expectations work seamlessly into the next.

References

Clark, R. E., Kirschner, P. A., & Sweller, J. (2012). Putting students on the path to learning: The case for fully guided instruction. *American Educator, 36*(1), 6–11.

Common Core State Standards for Mathematics. (n.d.). Retrieved June 1, 2011, from the Council of Chief State School Officers and National Governors Association website: http://corestandards.org/assets/CCSSI_Math%20Standards.pdf

Farran, D., Lipsey, M., Clements, D. H., Sarama, J., Hofer, K., Bilbrey, C., & Vorhaus, E. (2011). The mechanisms behind the results: Moderators of "building blocks" curricular effects. *Society for Research on Educational Effectiveness Abstracts,* 8–14.

Geary, D. C. (2004). Mathematics and learning disabilities. *Journal of Learning Disabilities, 37,* 4–15.

Mann, A., Moeller, K., Pixner, S., Kaufmann, L., & Nuerk, H.-C. (2011). Attentional strategies in place value integration: A longitudinal study on two-digit number comparison. *Journal of Psychology, 219*(1), 42–49.

National Center for Education Statistics. (2011). *The nation's report card.* Washington, DC: U.S. Department of Education. Available at http://nationsreportcard.gov/

National Mathematics Advisory Panel. (2008). *Foundations for success: The final report of the national mathematics advisory panel.* Washington, DC: U.S. Department of Education.

Riccomini, P. J., Witzel, B. S., & Riccomini, A. E. (2011). Maximize development in early childhood math programs by optimizing the instructional sequence. In N. L. Gallenstein & D. Hodges (Eds.), *Mathematics for all: Instructional strategies to assist students with learning challenges* (pp. 131–138). Olney, MD: ACEI.

Rosenshine, B. (2012). Principles of instruction: Research-based strategies that all teachers should know. *American Educator, 36*(1), 12–19, 39.

Witzel, B. S., & Riccomini, P. J. (2007). OPTIMIZE your curriculum for students with disabilities. *Preventing School Failure, 52*(1), 13–18.

Wu, H. (1999, Fall). Basic skills versus conceptual understanding: A bogus dichotomy in mathematics education. *American Educator,* 14–19, 50–52.

3

Assessment and Progress Monitoring of Number Sense

Assessments are the headlights of instruction. Without them you might make it to your destination, but you are much more likely to get lost.

Paul J. Riccomini

In this chapter, we present and discuss the purposes of assessments and the importance of properly assessing number sense in mathematics. We briefly discuss four common assessments used to evaluate number sense and provide examples of each. Additionally we discuss the importance of conducting error analysis procedures to pinpoint student error patterns to guide instruction. We will conclude with a brief discussion and description of the Race to the Top Assessment Program that is funding the development of a new Comprehensive Assessment System to be rolled out in 2014. After reading this chapter you will

1. recognize the four main purposes for assessing number sense.

2. recognize the different types of measures used to evaluate specific aspects of number sense.

3. recognize the importance of using error analysis procedures to inform instruction.

4. recognize the purpose of and subsequent challenges with new assessments currently under development.

Four Main Purposes of Assessments

Overall Outcomes Evaluation

The main purpose of the outcomes measures is to provide an overall evaluation of the effectiveness of the mathematics programs. This evaluation is generally based on preestablished performance levels (e.g., below basic, basic, proficiency, advanced). These outcomes assessments are mandated by federal and state guidelines and are often referred to as high-stakes assessments. The ramifications for not meeting expectations have brought a great deal of pressure to both teachers and students at all grade levels, especially third, fifth, and eighth grade. Although most outcome assessments do not include early elementary grades (i.e., Grades K–2), the pressure is mounting to improve early mathematics instructional programs as well.

These assessments are generally one-shot assessments that occur at or toward the end of the school year. The results are generally made available to the public and play a large part in the school and school district ratings. Since these assessments are used for overall evaluating purposes, the tests include materials taught throughout the course of the school year. Unfortunately, the results of these assessments are not necessarily instructionally useful to teachers. The results are usually not available until well after the school year has ended and students have moved on to the next grade level. With that said, these types of assessments are here to stay; the format and process may change (see "New Generation of Assessments" at the end of this chapter), but the accountability that is based on these results will likely continue to increase.

Screening

The purpose of screening measures is to provide teachers with an early warning system for students at risk for mathematics failure with the key phrase being *early warning.* The screening measures help identify students in need of additional instruction and subsequently further diagnosis. When teachers have early warning signs from screening measures, they are able to provide additional instruction to these students before the problem becomes significant.

Screening generally includes all students and is done near the beginning of the school year. Because all students are given the screening measures, it is imperative that the measures used are targeting critical areas that are predictive of overall mathematical achievement. If the screening measures have no predictive capacity, they should be revised or abandoned. The best screening tools have the strongest correlation to high-stakes assessments. Specific screening measures for measuring mathematical number sense are discussed later in this chapter.

Diagnostic

Diagnostic measures go beyond screening measures and provide more detailed information than outcomes assessments. Once a student has been identified by a screening measure as at risk, a diagnostic measure may help further detail the specific problem areas in mathematics in need of more intensive instruction. The information ascertained from a diagnostic assessment will better help teachers plan instruction because of the in-depth information about the student's skills and instructional needs it provides. This information may assist teachers in the identification of specific error patterns that students are exhibiting. When specific error patterns are identified, additional instruction can be much more targeted and ultimately more effective. More on error analysis is discussed at the end of this chapter.

Progress Monitoring

Progress monitoring is the frequent measuring of a student's rate of learning across time. Progress monitoring is used to determine if students are making adequate progress in the instructional program or need more intensive intervention to achieve grade-level mathematics outcomes. Progress monitoring and screening are foundational pillars in response-to-intervention (RTI) models currently gaining widespread popularity.

An important use of progress monitoring results is to determine if instructional programs and interventions are working. In RTI models, as students are identified as not making progress, additional instruction is delivered in the form of interventions. Five common measures of early numeracy that could be used with screening and progress monitoring are displayed in Figures 3a–3e. These common measures include quantification, numeral and number recognition, magnitude comparisons, counting strategies, and computation. Each of these early numeracy components, along with working memory and school engagement, has been used as a single measure or part of a series of measures to predict students' difficulties in mathematics learning (Gersten et al., 2012). Thus, students should be assessed early in key math and learning skills to determine instructional assistance and intensity of interventions.

Early Numeracy Measures

Quantity Array

Figure 3a Example Early Numeracy Assessment for Quantity Array

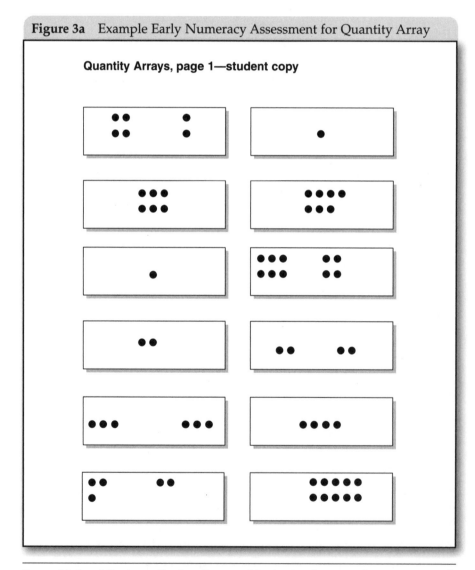

Source: National Center on Student Progress Monitoring (www.studentprogress.org).

Number Recognition

Figure 3b   Example Early Numeracy Assessment for Number
Identification

Number Identification, page 1—Student copy

12	17	5	5
34	13	3	10
37	45	20	13
45	64	31	12
23	10	17	47
17	49	58	1
14	23	6	23

Source: National Center on Student Progress Monitoring (www.studentprogress.org).

Magnitude Comparisons

Figure 3c   Example Early Assessment for Quantity Discrimination

Quantity discrimination, page 1—student copy

3 7	8 5	13 16
16 2	13 12	9 0
4 11	8 1	1 11
5 0	2 10	10 9
7 1	8 7	16 2
0 7	1 0	9 1
6 0	9 19	5 1

Source: National Center on Student Progress Monitoring (www.studentprogress.org).

Strategic Counting

Figure 3d   Example Early Assessment for Missing Number

Missing Number, page 3—student copy

5 __ 7 8	7 __ 9 10	__ 5 6 7
__ 8 9 10	3 4 5 __	2 3 __ 5
0 1 2 __	__ 2 3 4	1 2 __ 4
7 8 __ 10	1 2 3 __	__ 6 7 8
1 2 3 __	4 5 __ 7	70 80 90 __
3 __ 5 6	5 __ 7 8	3 4 5 __
12 14 __ 18	5 6 7 __	__ 8 9 10

Source: National Center on Student Progress Monitoring (www.studentprogress.org).

Fact Fluency

Figure 3e   Example Progress Monitoring Probe for Single Digit Multiplication Facts

0	0	5	8	4	8	4	7	0	6
×8	×5	×6	×7	×2	×7	×4	×3	×7	×9

9	7	2	5	7	4	3	6	9	8
×9	×1	×7	×4	×6	×8	×3	×7	×5	×3

- This type of probe can be administered once a week or every two weeks.
- Students have 2 minutes to write the correct answer to as many facts as possible.
- Teachers administer to all students and each student can graph their scores to see their progress.
- For students who are extremely slow writers, the probe can be administered orally.

- The purpose of this task for students is to increase (i.e., answer more facts correctly each time) the number of facts answered correctly.
- Teachers can use this type of probe to monitor students' progress in the memorization of their single digit multiplication facts.
- The progress monitoring probes are to be used in conjunction with regular practice between administering the probes

5	5	7	6	2	2	2	3	9	7
×3	×9	×4	×3	×6	×2	×1	×5	×4	×9

Goal: _____   **Number of problems correct:** _____

Every student will have an individually determined goal based on their writing speed.

Source: Adapted from Crawford (2003).

Error Pattern Analysis to Guide Instruction

When students struggle in mathematics, additional targeted interventions delivered through an instructional tiered approach are necessary to address students' learning needs. This approach is commonly referred to as response to intervention (Riccomini & Witzel, 2010).

Within this RTI approach, the level of instructional support and intensity increases with each tier, and student progress is monitored. In order for the system to function efficiently and effectively, the instruction and/or intervention implemented in each level must increase with intensity and be grounded in high-quality mathematics research. This approach has created great potential for improving and refining the instructional practices for teaching mathematics in general, but also to students who are struggling to achieve even basic levels of proficiency. The process of error analysis lends itself to the RTI framework in two ways. Error analysis is first individualized to specific student errors and second very intensive in nature; both are cornerstones to the RTI process.

Teachers investigate students' mathematical errors with the intent to improve instruction. It is not only instructionally helpful, but also essential, to evaluate individual students' work to determine an appropriate instructional focus to correct errors. The idea of providing corrective feedback and instruction is one of the main tenets of systematic and explicit instruction and should be considered for all students, but especially for students who are struggling in math. Regardless of students' ability levels, the identification and analysis of students' mathematical errors has the potential to improve the instructional planning by teachers. Error analysis is the systematic process by which teachers analyze students' worked-out solutions to mathematics problems with the purpose of identifying specific error patterns in order to provide appropriate corrective instruction.

The idea behind the interest in students' errors is in part driven by the belief that it is not possible to fix something until you know it is broken. Without knowing students' errors, it's impossible to provide appropriate instruction. It's kind of like driving a car without headlights in the dark. You might make it, and you might not!

Conducting Error Analysis

There are four steps to the process of analyzing students' worked-out solutions. The process includes the following: (1) collect students' completed independent work, (2) analyze and identify errors and/or error patterns, (3) develop a corrective instruction plan, and (4) evaluate the student. We will discuss each step in more detail. Keep in mind that many teachers probably complete some if not all of these steps, but I am recommending that this becomes more systematic and routine, especially in the context of RTI. This means all of those organizational strategies that teachers use should be employed for record keeping.

Step 1: Collect students' completed independent work. In order to have a good representative sample of students' work, the work should be across a couple of days or assignments. The point often overlooked is that the work needs to be independent work. Mathematical assessments discussed at the beginning of this chapter are almost always independent and therefore make excellent sources of student work for error analysis. Progress monitoring assessments can provide teachers with an excellent sample of student work because progress monitoring assessments are given more frequently, sometimes once a week. There is one caveat to using progress monitoring measures, and that is the lack of problem formats repeated. Progress monitoring is often a broad sampling of the mathematics curriculum, so there might only be one or two problems. That's why it's important to use several samples of a student's independent work for error analysis across a period of time, maybe one to two weeks. After you have collected a representative sample of students' work, it's time to start analyzing the solutions. Just a quick note: Keeping students' work organized in individual student folders can help facilitate the next steps.

Step 2: Analyze and identify errors and/or error patterns. This is the most important step and requires the most amount of attention and organization. The analysis of solutions can start with the answer, but must involve the actual worked-out steps. Keep in mind that, in mathematics, incorrect procedures can still result in a correct answer. If you only examine incorrect answers, it is quite possible that you will not identify an underlying error. Examining students' worked-out solutions can be very helpful, but you are not necessarily able to determine what they are thinking. Sometimes an interview is applicable in this step. Examining paper-and-pencil solutions has its limitations, but when combined with selective interviewing, the result can be a very powerful instructional tool.

When analyzing the solutions, we are trying to specifically identify the error. Simply identifying a problem type is not sufficient. For example, you may see that a student has missed every problem involving the subtraction with regrouping. Although this description might be instructionally helpful, it doesn't clearly identify the error. A carefully conducted error analysis may actually reveal the student is only missing subtraction problems that involve regrouping across a zero, a very common error pattern in subtraction (Ashlock, 2010). So, based on the students' specific errors, the teacher plans individual corrective instruction for each student accordingly.

Step 3: Develop a corrective instruction plan. After the error is pinpointed, a corrective instruction plan can be developed. The options that teachers can use to provide additional targeted instruction to correct errors are rather expansive and depend entirely on the strengths and weaknesses of the student. Many of these options are covered in great detail across the chapters in this book; however, there are a few basic guidelines to consider. First, confirm that the student has the necessary preskill/precursor skills to complete the larger problem. Second, develop demonstration examples, guided practice examples, and independent practice problems. As a general rule, I recommend developing between three and four problems for each phase. Finally, the corrective instruction should be explicit and systematic.

Step 4: Evaluate the student. After the corrective instruction is delivered, it is essential to determine if the error pattern has been corrected. This can be done in several ways. First, if you are progress monitoring the student, a careful review of the problem type and error targeted for corrective instruction can be completed using two to three of the progress monitoring measures. Second, you can develop a mini-assessment of the specific skill or concept that was targeted. Lastly, it might be helpful to verbally assess the student by asking the student to explain the problem solution. No matter the process, it is vital to determine if the error was corrected.

It is important to identify the specific error that is occurring, and once the pattern is identified, teachers are better prepared to provide specific corrective instruction for the student (Ashlock, 2010; Riccomini, 2005). If the error is not identified and verified by the teacher, additional targeted instruction may not target the correct misconception, which will not help the student. As well, providing additional instruction without first identifying the student error patterns is inefficient and wastes valuable instructional time.

New Generation of Assessments

In 2009, the U.S. Congress funded the Race to the Top Assessment Program. The main purpose of this program was to develop a "new generation" of assessments to better serve the public. The program provided funding to two consortia of states to develop a Comprehensive Assessment System (CAS). The consortia are charged with developing a new assessment system that will accomplish four main goals: (1) provide more well-timed data, (2) provide data that can support and inform instruction, (3) provide a more accurate measure of what students have learned and can do, and (4) measure student achievement on standards that link to the skills and knowledge required for success in college and the workforce (Educational Testing Service, 2012). Clearly, the two consortia have significant challenges ahead of them as they look to redefine educational assessments.

The two consortia are the Partnership for Assessment of Readiness for College and Careers (PARCC; www.parcconline.org) and the Smarter Balanced Assessment Consortium (www.smarterbalanced .org). Currently, 45 states and the District of Columbia have joined the consortia, hence agreeing to the adoption of the newly developed CAS as their main evaluative tool. Each consortium has a timeline in which information, professional development, and actual test items will be released. Unfortunately, this is happening at lightning speed with the assessments going to place in 2014, thus leaving very little time for teachers to truly prepare for the CAS. We encourage all educators and parents to become familiar with the assessments as soon as more information is released.

The two consortia have committed to the construction of the CAS for Grades 3–8, and high school will have four common themes. First, and arguably most important, the CAS will be based on common standards for mathematics and English language arts (ELA). Proponents of the common standards maintain that the Common Core State Standards (CCSS) differ from current standards because the primary focus is in the area of college- and career-readiness knowledge and skills. Second, the CAS will aim to measure student growth compared to current assessments that are more summative in nature. A common criticism on current state assessments is they do not account for student growth because they are administered one time at the end of the year. Besides student growth in mathematics and ELA, the measures are designed to evaluate proficiency. Third, the assessments will provide a reliable indication to determine if students are on track at each grade level as well as indicate the students' preparedness for college and/or career readiness. Finally, and most important for educators, is the idea that the CAS will provide useful and practical information in a timely fashion to help educations make informed decisions about their teaching, curricular materials, and student learning. Additionally, the CAS will form the main evaluative piece in the determination of the principal and teacher effectiveness (Educational Testing Services, 2012).

Critical Issues for Educators

At the time of this book, specific information pertaining to assessments is not available, and therefore it is not possible to fully describe and realize the implications for early mathematics instruction. Much of the information provided here is from the K–12 Center at ETS (www .k12center.org). As more and more information is released, educators will have a better idea of the impacts to curricular materials, teaching, and student learning. Instead on focusing on trying to describe assessments that are not yet developed, we will focus on three important considerations to help better prepare educators for the new CAS.

First, it is critical that all K–2 teachers are included in the professional development opportunities for Grades 3–8 teachers relating to information about the new CAS. Even though there is not a requirement (at least at this point) for assessments in grades K–2, it is absolutely vital for K–2 teachers to understand the testing expectations required of their students starting in Grade 3. This idea is especially important in mathematics, maybe more than any other content area. If K–2 teachers are not fully knowledgeable in the type of tasks expected of upper-middle elementary students, they cannot begin to facilitate the higher-level thinking that is the cornerstone of the new assessments. It is essential for K–2 educators to construct a solid and comprehensive foundation for later success in mathematics.

Second, states and districts should begin to develop and/or refine current K–2 assessments that mirror and align with the expectations of the new assessments. Although the PARCC is developing a K–2 assessment that is optional and will no doubt cost money, over the past several years huge amounts of money and time have been invested in finding, developing, and refining various assessments for Grades K–2. These assessments were used for multiple reasons such as RTI models, district benchmarks, evaluative purposes, predicting state standards, and so on, but because the new generation of assessments will be drastically different, it is yet to be determined if the current assessments will have any direct link to the new assessments. It is certainly a "learn as we go" time in education as it relates to the CCSS assessments. It is of the utmost importance that the K–2 assessments used by schools and districts properly align with these new statewide assessments.

A final and larger question relating to the new assessments lies with the two main types of assessments currently used in all RTI models, universal screening and progress monitoring. Remember that the purpose of universal screeners and progress monitoring measures is first to identify students at risk for academic failure and then to progress monitor those students on their rate of growth toward end-of-year goals. Given that there are now "newly revised" end-of-year goals in mathematics (i.e., CCSS) and a "new generation" of assessments, at this point it is not known if the universal screeners or progress monitoring measures will indeed have any predictive power. A main tenet of progress monitoring is that the data help teachers make decisions regarding end-of-year outcomes. If there is not a strong connection, the progress monitoring measures will have to be reevaluated. Again, this is probably more of an issue with mathematics than with reading, but certainly should be a concern for those involved in a RTI framework. As the new assessments become available and put to use, educators must carefully analyze the link between currently used assessments in Grades K–2 and the new assessments.

Clearly, the new assessments hold a great deal of promise for providing educators with more useful and timely information that can be used to inform instructional and curricular decisions. Additionally, the new assessments may offer an improved method to measure what students can actually do versus what they cannot, but it is certainly an anxious time as we all await the unveiling of the new generation of assessments.

Conclusion

The wealth of information regarding student mathematical performance that can be ascertained from the various assessments is essential to providing more targeted instruction; however, data are only part of the picture. Examining students' actual worked-out solution through a systematic process to identify specific error patterns is vital to more effective instruction. Mathematical problems may be missed because of carelessness, computational fact error, component skill error, and/or strategy errors. As students learn more advanced applications of concepts and skills, the problems can be caused by any combination of the four error categories. This complexity in student errors requires teachers to implement systematic error analysis procedures regularly, but this approach is essential for students with disabilities.

Additional Resources

More specific and detailed information pertaining to the research background, administration, scoring procedures, and decision making of various early numeracy assessments can be found in Table 3.1.

Table 3.1   Information Pertaining to the Various Early Numeracy Assessments

Organization	*Web Address*
National Center on Student Progress Monitoring	www.studentprogress.org
Research Institute on Progress Monitoring	www.progressmonitoring.org
National Research Center on Learning Disabilities	www.nrcld.org
Division for Learning Disabilities of the Council for Exceptional Children	www.teachingld.org
National Center on Response to Intervention	www.rti4success.org
Intervention Central	www.interventioncentral.org
Center on Instruction	www.centeroninstruction.org
The IRIS Center for Training Enhancements	http://iris.peabody.vanderbilt.edu
The Access Center: Improving Outcomes for All Students K–8	www.k8accesscenter.org
Center on Positive Behavioral Interventions and Supports (PBIS)	www.pbis.org
Partnership for Assessment of Readiness for College and Careers (PARCC)	http://parcconline.org
Smarter Balanced Assessment Consortium	www.smarterbalanced.org

Source: Adapted from Berkeley & Riccomini (2011).

References

Ashlock, R. B. (2010). *Error patterns in computation: Using error patterns to help each student learn* (10th ed.). Upper Saddle River, NJ: Pearson Education.

Berkeley, S., & Riccomini, P. J. (2011). Academic progress monitoring. In J. M. Kauffman & D. P. Hallahan (Eds.), *Handbook of special education* (pp. 334–347). New York: Routledge.

Crawford, D. B. (2003). *Mastering math facts: Blackline masters and answer keys.* Eau Claire, WI: Otter Creek Institute.

Educational Testing Service. (2012, April). *Coming together to raise achievement: New assessments for the common core state standards.* Center for K–12

Assessment & Performance Management at ETS. Retrieved April 7, 2012, from http://www.k12center.org/rsc/pdf/Coming_Together_April_2012_Final.PDF

Gersten, R., Clarke, B., Jordan, N. C., Newman-Gonchar, R., Haymond, K., & Wilkins, C. (2012). Universal screening in mathematics for the primary grades: Beginnings of a research base. *Exceptional Children, 78*(4), 423–445.

Riccomini, P. J. (2005). Identification and remediation of systematic error patterns in subtraction. *Learning Disability Quarterly, 28*(3), 1–10.

Riccomini, P. J., & Witzel, B. S. (2010). *Response to intervention in math.* Thousand Oaks, CA: Corwin.

4

Counting, Number Identification, and Early Addition and Subtraction

Before I place my children to sleep, I always tell them that I love them. One night, my 6-year-old says "I love you" first. I reply, "Oh, I love you more." She comes back with "I love you infinity!" I laugh and say, "I love you infinity plus one." With a knowing smirk, she replies, "Ha! You can't go beyond infinity. Don't you know the number line? See, I win!"

Before school formally begins, many students already know about counting. However, counting is done in a singsong fashion. Students will count by rote from "one" to a specific number followed by an adult's praise. Rote counting is a satisfactory start, but it is merely a verbal representation of a string of numbers presented in series formation. Success in rote counting is largely associated with working memory and not necessarily students' knowledge of numbers. Students have been presented with numbers orally from "one" to "ten" or maybe "one" to "twenty" without clear indication of seriation. More is needed.

Compare learning to count with learning the alphabet. Students often first hear the alphabet through the alphabet song sung to the melody of "Twinkle, Twinkle, Little Star." Students sing the song willingly and with enthusiasm. It has a catchy beat and is a preschool favorite. Through this song, children learn some common letter names such as "ay," "bee," "see," and "dee," as well as some uncommon ones, such as "elemenno." The letters in the alphabet song are sometimes even taught according to the order in which they are sung. In K–12 schools, many of us may remember playing vocabulary games where we are given points for words by adding letters that are assigned values according to where the letter is presented in the alphabet song, a *b* meaning 2. Contrast this to counting. Where the alphabet does not have a specified and purposeful order, numbers do. Children are taught the order of the letters, which are more arbitrarily sequenced. However, children are more likely to know the sequence of letters than numbers, which have a specified and purposeful order. To make matters worse, some educators argue that the alphabet song incorrectly sets up parents and ill-prepared educators to present letters in a poorly designed sequence. Nonetheless, most students grow up learning the alphabet as it is sung in a pattern matching the popular song. For numbers, however, their order is not set to a popular song or rhyme and thus is practiced far less than the alphabet. We urge educators to teach the order of numbers and practice this order often, especially with young children.

It is difficult to separate counting, numeral and number identification, and early addition and subtraction because of the implicit association between these number sense components. However, it is important to examine how children develop early understandings of each. At an early age, most children develop a sense of *more* and *less* as shown when comparing quantities, such as number of cookies. When two children are given different numbers of cookies, they will compare how many one child has in a 1:1 relation to the other child. This relation comes before formal and consistent counting (Krasa & Shunkwiler, 2009). Using the idea of comparisons and relations, children may be taught to count as a means of comparison. Not only should children learn to rotely count accurately and consistently at an early age, but they should also learn to extend counting from a given number and even be able to indicate what number comes before a given number. In what may be called a mental number line, children should be able to visualize and understand the sequence of numbers. Once the sequence is understood, children should be able to recognize connected numerals to the words they are saying. However, number knowledge goes well beyond rote counting and numeral recognition. Number knowledge includes knowing the magnitude and value of numbers, and counting principles extending well through operational skills. In this chapter, we emphasize aspects of counting and provide how to teach those aspects as they set up addition and subtraction. We also explain how standards, specifically the Common Core State Standards (CCSS), progress from one grade level to the next in developing counting as it relates to early operational skills (see Table 4.1).

Key aspects of the chapter:

1. Teach rote counting to build seriation and interest.

2. Teach numeral connections to the numbers used in rote counting.

3. Assign value and magnitude of number to show an increasing size of number. There are warnings here as well since number is not always one or the other.

4. Use counting principles to work across the number line and with concrete objects to teach addition and subtraction.

5. Build fluency and automaticity of addition and subtraction.

Counting

"As students use more effective, efficient counting strategies to solve basic arithmetic combinations, they reinforce their conceptual understanding of important mathematical principles (e.g., commutativity and the associative law)" (Gersten, Clarke, Haymond, & Jordan, 2011, p. 7).

Counting is an exercise in sequential number naming that should eventually build to a mental visualization of a number line. Visualizing a number line should start with whole numbers from 0 and extend to the right or upward. Students will then develop this mental number line to include rational numbers such as integers to the left or downward from the 0 and then fractions or decimals between each integer. This development occurs from kindergarten throughout elementary and into secondary school.

In the CCSS, there are numerous mentions of counting in the kindergarten section. This work on counting prepares students for addition and subtraction in first grade. In kindergarten counting

Table 4.1 CCSS Related to Counting Development

Number Sense Component	Kindergarten	First Grade	Second Grade	Third Grade
Counting Principles	K.CC.1. Count to 100 by ones and by tens. K.CC.2. Count forward beginning from a given number within the known sequence (instead of having to begin at 1). K.CC.5. Count to answer "how many?" questions about as many as 20 things arranged in a line, a rectangular array, or a circle, or as many as 10 things in a scattered configuration; given a number from 1–20, count out that many objects.	**Extend the counting sequence.** 1.NBT.1. Count to 120, starting at any number less than 120. In this range, read and write numerals and represent a number of objects with a written numeral.	2.NBT.2. Count within 1,000; skip-count by 5s, 10s, and 100s.	Number and Operations—Fractions* 3.NF **Develop understanding of fractions as numbers.** 2. Understand a fraction as a number on the number line; represent fractions on a number line diagram. a. Represent a fraction 1/b on a number line diagram by defining the interval from 0 to 1 as the whole and partitioning it into b equal parts. Recognize that each part has size 1/b and that the endpoint of the part based at 0 locates the number 1/b on the number line. b. Represent a fraction a/b on a number line diagram by marking off a lengths 1/b from 0. Recognize that the resulting interval has size a/b and that its endpoint locates the number a/b on the number line.

* *Note:* Grade 3 expectations in this domain are limited to fractions with denominators 2, 3, 4, 6, and 8.

Source: Standards found at http://www.corestandards.org/assets/CCSSI_Math%20Standards.pdf

standards work across counting and cardinality while in first grade it is called number and operations in base 10. Counting then extends to more complex skip counting in second grade to prepare students for multiplication. In third grade, counting principles include fractions, which extend to integers and to a coordinate plane in successive grades. This sequence differs from our suggested one above. Through our work internationally, we recognize that in many countries where Celsius is used to express temperature, many preschoolers are exposed to negative numbers in preschool settings. While integers are introduced in U.S. curricula in late elementary to early middle school levels, students can understand and work with integers much earlier.

Beginning Counting

Students who come to school knowing the sequence of numbers in counting have a distinct advantage. This does not mean that they will be mathematically superior by the end of kindergarten, but it certainly provides them with an opportunity of advancement.

While many students may have memorized the alphabet song, far fewer have memorized a song for number counting. Choose a song to help students get started. Counting songs, like the one by Jack Hartmann (http://www.songsforteaching.com/jackhartmann/counting1to20.htm), help students learn the order of the numbers. Start with counting to "five" on a single hand, and then count to "ten" by using both hands. A focus on computation needs to focus on sums (4 + 6) and minuends (10 − 6) of 10.

4 + 6 totals 10

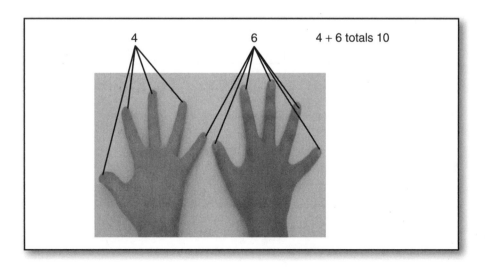

Counting to and from "ten" is essential as a precursor skill. Once this sequence is memorized, grow to "fifty" and then "one hundred." When children are beginning to count, using physical objects such as balls, chips, counters, and fingers is useful. However, students need to learn that counting is not always with physical objects. When counting is only with physical objects, children tend to start with the number 1 representing one item. It is important to teach students that 0 comes before 1 and that 1, itself, may represent a distance between 0 and 1. The distance concept is important as it prepares students for use of a number line for addition and subtraction and eventually with measurement and rational numbers. Once single-digit counting is memorized, then students should begin working on multiples using a skip counting technique. To teach multiples, a 100s grid can be used to show how we are counting by 10s such that 10 represents one 10, 20 represents two 10s, 30 represents three 10s, and eventually 100 represents ten 10s. Figure 4.1 is a 100s grid for counting and skip counting that begins with 0.

Figure 4.1   100s Grid for Counting and Skip Counting

0	1	2	3	4	5	6	7	8	9
10	11	12	13	14	15	16	17	18	19
20	21	22	23	24	25	26	27	28	29
30	31	32	33	34	35	36	37	38	39
40	41	42	43	44	45	46	47	48	49
50	51	52	53	54	55	56	57	58	59
60	61	62	63	64	65	66	67	68	69
70	71	72	73	74	75	76	77	78	79
80	81	82	83	84	85	86	87	88	89
90	91	92	93	94	95	96	97	98	99

Strategic Counting

By the time most children enter school, they have formed the basic understanding of arithmetic counting to form addition and subtraction and are beginning to develop memory-based processes

Figure 4.2   This student uses coins to count by 5s and 10s.

(Geary, Hoard, Nugent, & Byrd-Craven, 2007). Extending their understanding through use of number lines helps provide children with a visual of frequently used strategies, counting on or forward from a given number and counting back from a given number. In the example below, the teacher asks students to count four more than 3. The students place their finger on 3 and then count on four more numbers while moving their hands to the right on the number line (4, 5, 6, 7). Finish with "three plus four is seven." Since students learned to start with "zero" in their counting, they will not make the mistake of saying "one" when starting at 3 and erroneously ending at 6.

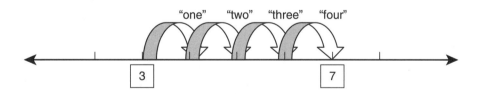

In the first grade students should begin to develop a mental number line, and by second grade they should be counting up to 1,000 using multiples of 5, 10, and 100 as they develop place value. The development of a mental number line is essential to future mathematics. Just as counting is to be understood early as a distance between two numbers on a number line, in the third grade the introduction to rational numbers should precede the mental understanding of a number line.

One of the more complex math concepts historically is fractions and decimals. The complexity was obviously not lost on those who wrote the CCSS for mathematics. Even the first fractions standard in the third grade may be hard to understand. Fractions are written as a numerator over a denominator where the denominator indicates the number of equal parts needed to make one whole. The numerator is the number of denominator-sized movements along a number line. Thus, $\frac{2}{5}$ means that each one whole is broken into five equal parts and this fraction is the size of two of them. Likewise, $\frac{7}{4}$ means that each one whole is broken into four equal parts and this fraction is the size of seven of those parts. This initial understanding of fractions is important to developing conceptual and computational reasoning. While most of us might try to infer that this lengthy definition is essentially saying a part of a whole, it is really meant to establish the notion that "fractions are numbers and they expand the number system beyond whole numbers" (Siegler et al., 2010, p. 19). In the Institute of Education Sciences practice guide *Developing Effective Fractions Instruction for Kindergarten Through 8th Grade,* Siegler and his colleagues (2010) explain many misconceptions of computation of fractions and how these errors are often rooted in misunderstandings that fractions have magnitudes just like whole numbers, which are so much more familiar to young students.

To help students understand that fractions have magnitude, show how a fraction can be represented as a point on a number line. Space out the distance between each point according to the denominator, and then mark where the numerator is accordingly. Since a fraction is simply a number represented by one whole number divided by another, a number line is an ideal starting place. For the large number of students who require concrete connections when learning, use fraction strips and other linear means of showing what a fraction ultimately stands for.

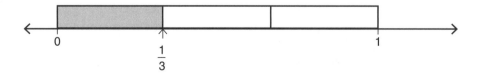

Number Identification

"Just as letter-naming accuracy and speed predict a child's ability to benefit from typical reading instruction, numeral recognition, measured in early screenings, may identify students with possible difficulties in mathematics" (Gersten, Clarke, Haymond, & Jordan, 2011, p. 8).

Students who are knowledgeable of or even familiar with numerals have a vocabulary advantage, both written and verbal, over their peers. Numeral recognition means to connect a numeral with a number of items. Number recognition includes not only numeral recognition but cardinality as well. This is a fairly brief part of the CCSS but important in that it works with the mental number line and every calculation problem to come (see Table 4.2). Creating a mental number line during counting instruction builds understanding of numerical magnitude. "Children's understanding of numerical magnitudes is closely related to their general math achievement" (Laski & Siegler, 2007, p. 1723). Teaching number magnitude should be pervasive across counting and place value.

Table 4.2   CCSS Related to Numeral and Number Recognition

Numeral and Number Recognition	K.CC.3. Write numbers from 0 to 20. Represent a number of objects with a written numeral 0–20 (with 0 representing a count of no objects). K.CC.4. Understand the relationship between numbers and quantities; connect counting to cardinality.	1.NBT.1. Counting is to 120. In this range, read and write numerals and represent a number of objects with a written numeral.

Source: Standards found at http://www.corestandards.org/assets/CCSSI_Math%20 Standards.pdf

Teach Number Recognition

Students must be able to write numerals from 0 to 9 in order to effectively communicate numbers on paper. Make the formation accurate in development by focusing on a top-down approach that starts at a single point in the top left or top middle of a defined space for writing. See *Letters and Numbers for Me* (Olson, 2008) for examples of this formation. To form the numerals, a writing utensil and paper may be used, but so can an index finger and a cookie sheet with rice, salt, or shaving cream. It is important to have students practice the formation. In order to have them remember the pattern of each numeral, share rhymes or memorable sayings. For some examples, see the list in Figure 4.3 from Riccomini and Witzel (2010). Once 0–9 are mastered, using place value knowledge (see Chapter 5) students should begin forming two-digit numbers.

Figure 4.3   Rhymes and Sayings for Remembering the Pattern of Numerals 0–9

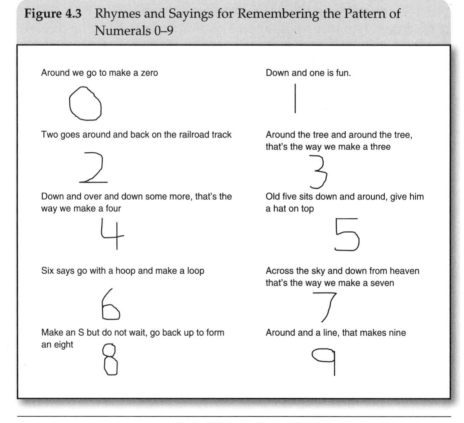

Around we go to make a zero

Down and one is fun.

Two goes around and back on the railroad track

Around the tree and around the tree, that's the way we make a three

Down and over and down some more, that's the way we make a four

Old five sits down and around, give him a hat on top

Six says go with a hoop and make a loop

Across the sky and down from heaven that's the way we make a seven

Make an S but do not wait, go back up to form an eight

Around and a line, that makes nine

Source: Riccomini and Witzel (2010). Reprinted with permission.

Once basic numeral recognition is understood, teachers can extend recognition from work to place value understanding and work on number recognition. For example, it is important to communicate 43 as "forty-three," but it is more important to identify the magnitude of the number as four 10s plus three 1s. For more information on multiple-digit numbers, see Chapter 5.

Link Counting and Cardinality

Numeral recognition involves simple identification of the name of a number per the abstract numeral. Number recognition connects that name to a number of objects. Knowing the name of a symbolic numeral solely involves memory, which may be taught and practiced through a number of means, such as repetition and practice or teaching cueing. Connecting a numeral to a magnitude or value of number involves more processing. This is called cardinality, and it involves quick or automatic recognition of a number of objects. In order for a student to explain this recognition, however, she must already know the numeral that connects to the number and have mastered counting small groups of objects. To check a student's cardinality, show him or her a small number of objects and see if each is immediately named without counting. Any hesitation or eye movement gives away a lack of cardinality per that number. A general rule is to not show more items than the student's age or more than six objects. Also, displaying objects in close proximity is easier because of a young person's tight field of vision.

This is a valuable skill for developing addition and subtraction strategies because of efficiency. Students who count the first addend to every addition problem and then count the second addend often add them by counting them over again starting with "one."

The problem reads:

4 + 3 =

Without Cardinality

The student places four objects down and says, "One, two, three, four."

Then the student places three objects down for the second addend and says, "One, two, three."

Finally, the student recognizes the addition symbol and adds the objects by counting, "One, two, three, four, five, six, seven. The answer is seven."

With Cardinality

Instead, a student who has developed appropriate cardinality will lay down four and say, "Four," and then lay down three more and count them as he lays them down: "Five, six, seven." Recognizing he has laid down three more, he says, "The answer is seven."

This same developed cardinality is even more effective in subtraction problems.

The problem reads:

6 − 2 =

Without Cardinality

Students who have not developed their cardinality may lay down six objects while counting them: "One, two, three, four, five, six."

Recognizing the subtraction symbol, the student may view it as "take away" and pull two out: "One, two." To find the answer, the student again counts the remaining items: "One, two, three, four. The answer is four."

With Cardinality

Instead, a student who has developed appropriate cardinality will lay down six and say, "Six," and then pull out two. Recognizing that four remain, he will say, "The answer is four."

To help build cardinality, practice identifying small quantities of objects in different orientations and have the students quickly name their magnitude. You can even connect those objects to a number line to show how they represent the same value.

Intervention for Students Struggling With Counting and Cardinality

For students struggling with cardinality, start with rote counting from "zero." Use a song to create a counting rhythm or at least a sing-song tone while counting. Count often. Once counting is established, show the numerals in correct order, connected while counting. Stop the counting midstream and ask students to point to the number that was last said. For cardinality, start with groups of two objects in close proximity before increasing the number. If students can reliably subitize up to four objects, then begin more complex configurations.

Early Addition and Subtraction

"Researchers (Goldman, Pellegrino, & Mertz, 1988; Hasselbring, Goin, & Bransford, 1988) consistently found that struggling elementary students could not retrieve addition and subtraction number combinations automatically" (Gersten, Clarke, Haymond, & Jordan, 2011, p. 7).

It is important for students to understand and be automatic in addition and subtraction. Teachers have linked difficulties learning multiplication, long division, and computation of rational numbers to knowledge of addition and subtraction. Thus, significant amounts of preparation, instructional time, and practice must be dedicated to teaching addition and subtraction as more than "put together" and "take away." Addition and subtraction must be understood as directions on a number line, and single-digit operations should be practiced until automatically recalled both verbally and orthographically.

Gersten, Clarke, Haymond, and Jordan (2011) emphasized the need for students to understand and retrieve basic combinations of arithmetic. They found that students with mathematics difficulties typically lack semantic memory required to automatically recall facts. To relieve some of the memorization load required for developing automaticity, it is important to focus on properties of addition, particularly the commutative property. Once memorized, addition and subtraction should be applied to other mathematics such as measurement, multiplication, and rational numbers.

The CCSS set up addition and subtraction across several grades. In kindergarten, the learning starts with concrete objects, computation about 10, and fluency of minuends and sums to 5. The most

Table 4.3 CCSS Related to Addition and Subtraction

K.OA.1. Represent addition and subtraction with objects, fingers, mental images, drawings[1], sounds (e.g., claps), acting out situations, verbal explanations, expressions, or equations.	1.OA.1	Increase in application of facts	Operations and Algebraic Thinking 3.OA
	Represent and solve problems involving addition and subtraction.	**Operations and Algebraic Thinking 2.OA.1**	**Solve problems involving the four operations, and identify and explain patterns in arithmetic.**
	1. Use addition and subtraction within 20 to solve word problems involving situations of adding to, taking from, putting together, taking apart, and comparing, with unknowns in all positions, e.g., by using objects, drawings, and equations with a symbol for the unknown number to represent the problem.	**Represent and solve problems involving addition and subtraction.**	8. Solve two-step word problems using the four operations. Represent these problems using equations with a letter standing for the unknown quantity. Assess the reasonableness of answers using mental computation and estimation strategies including rounding.[3]
K.OA.3. Decompose numbers less than or equal to 10 into pairs in more than one way, e.g., by using objects or drawings, and record each decomposition by a drawing or equation (e.g., $5 = 2 + 3$ and $5 = 4 + 1$).	1.OA.3	1. Use addition and subtraction within 100 to solve one- and two-step word problems involving situations of adding to, taking from, putting together, taking apart, and comparing, with unknowns in all positions, e.g., by using drawings and equations with a symbol for the unknown number to represent the problem.	9. Identify arithmetic patterns (including patterns in the addition table or multiplication table), and explain them using properties of operations.
	Apply properties of operations as strategies to add and subtract. *Examples: If $8 + 3 = 11$ is known, then $3 + 8 = 11$ is also known. (Commutative property of addition.) To add $2 + 6 + 4$, the second two numbers can be added to make a ten, so $2 + 6 + 4 = 2 + 10 = 12$. (Associative property of addition.)*	**Add and subtract within 20.**	*For example, observe that 4 times a number is always even, and explain why 4 times a number can be decomposed into two equal addends.*
	1.OA.4	2. Fluently add and subtract within 20 using mental strategies.[2] By end of Grade 2, know from memory all sums of two one-digit numbers.	
K.OA.4. For any number from 1 to 9, find the number that makes 10 when added to the given number, e.g., by using objects or drawings, and record the answer with a drawing or equation.	Understand subtraction as an unknown-addend problem. *For example, subtract $10 - 8$ by finding the number that makes 10 when added to 8.*	4. Use addition to find the total number of objects arranged in rectangular arrays with up to 5 rows and up to 5 columns; write an equation to express the total as a sum of equal addends.	
	Add and subtract within 20.		
K.OA.5. Fluently add and subtract within 5.	1.OA.5. Relate counting to addition and subtraction (e.g., by counting on 2 to add 2).		
	1.OA.6. Add and subtract within 20, demonstrating fluency for addition and subtraction within 10. Use strategies such as counting on; making ten (e.g., $8 + 6 = 8 + 2 + 4 =$		

	Relate addition and subtraction to length.
$10 + 4 = 14$); decomposing a number leading to a ten (e.g., $13 - 4 = 13 - 3 - 1 = 10 - 1 = 9$); using the relationship between addition and subtraction (e.g., knowing that $8 + 4 = 12$, one knows $12 - 8 = 4$); and creating equivalent but easier or known sums (e.g., adding $6 + 7$ by creating the known equivalent $6 + 6 + 1 = 12 + 1 = 13$).	2.MD.5. Use addition and subtraction within 100 to solve word problems involving lengths that are given in the same units, e.g., by using drawings (such as drawings of rulers) and equations with a symbol for the unknown number to represent the problem.
Work with addition and subtraction equations.	
1.OA.7. Understand the meaning of the equal sign, and determine if equations involving addition and subtraction are true or false. *For example, which of the following equations are true and which are false? $6 = 6, 7 = 8 - 1, 5 + 2 = 2 + 5, 4 + 1 = 5 + 2$.*	2.MD.6. Represent whole numbers as lengths from 0 on a number line diagram with equally spaced points corresponding to the numbers 0, 1, 2, . . . , and represent whole-number sums and differences within 100 on a number line diagram.
1.OA.8. Determine the unknown whole number in an addition or subtraction equation relating three whole numbers. *For example, determine the unknown number that makes the equation true in each of the equations $8 + ? = 11, 5 = \square - 3, 6 + 6 = \square$.*	

Notes:

1. Drawings need not show details, but should show the mathematics in the problem.

2. See Standard 1.OA.6 for a list of mental strategies.

3. This standard is limited to problems posed with whole numbers and having whole-number answers; students should know how to perform operations in the conventional order when there are no parentheses to specify a particular order (Order of Operations).

Source: Standards found at http://www.corestandards.org/assets/CCSSI_Math%20Standards.pdf

intense grade for working on addition and subtraction is first grade. In the first grade, students must learn computation within 20, use of properties, and problem solving using unknowns. By second grade, addition and subtraction fluency within 20 is expected, and the application spreads to multistep word problems and measurement as related to word problems. In third grade, application expands to multiplication and mixed operations word problems.

Kindergarten

Addition and subtraction computation starts quickly in formal schooling. In kindergarten, organize basic addition and subtraction around the concrete to representational to abstract (CRA) sequence of instruction. Start computation using similar physical movements and manipulatives to what the students used to learn counting, numeral-to-number connections, and cardinality. While manipulating objects to complete addition and subtraction equations, have students explain their reasoning. Show expressions and equations with accurate vocabulary, such as *equal* meaning "is the same as." This standard may be used to set up addition and subtraction reasoning and interest. Using hands as a key concrete manipulative, teach students to pull apart numbers. Start by breaking apart 5 as an answer to addition of 4 and 1, 2 and 3, or 5 and 0. Use counting on or up for addition and counting down for subtraction. Transition from hands to pictorial representations, such as one row of a ten frame or drawings of objects. Finally, connect the pictorial representations to abstract equations. Once addition is understood, make connections back to subtraction connecting concrete manipulations to abstract equation solving.

Concrete	Pictorial Representation	Abstract
▲▲▲ + ▲▲	△△△ + △△	3 + 2 = 5

After groups of five, begin to concentrate instruction around groups of ten. A clear way to build this is through the CRA sequence of instruction. Start with a concrete representation, such as fingers. Use both hands, as shown early in counting, to build from cardinality to equation naming, such as 7 + 3 = 10. Once students can represent multiple decompositions of 10 on their fingers, show the combinations using a ten frame. The goal is the abstract understanding of decomposition of 10.

7 + 3 is the same as 10

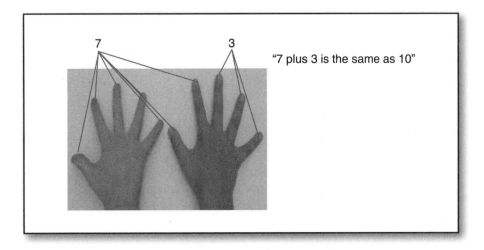

Ten frame of 7 + 3 is the same as 10

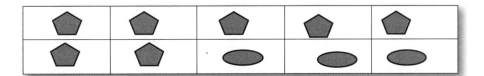

Once students learn the reasoning and accuracy, they should memorize addition and subtraction within 5. This memorization should be taken to fluency with both verbal rehearsal and written practice. Make a goal of 20 problems per minute using verbal rehearsal. Setting expectations of written problems per minute should be limited with young children. Children have different levels of fine motor coordination to complete an orthographic set of problems whether written or multiple choice selected on a computer. Although many people may think that memorization is only through "Drill and Kill," not that I ever understood that, practice can be done in several ways—from paired groups, to flash cards, to worksheets, to clapping games, to puzzles, to coloring pictures. It is important not to state or act like practice is ineffective or "beneath" someone. In fact, practice is part of most expertise and will hopefully be a part of every student's future.

Figure 4.4

First Grade

In the first grade, the maximum minuend and sum increase to 20. The multiple scenarios used in kindergarten are now presented in the written form of word problems. This progression of problem solving is presented across grade levels. The language of the word problems should be used both verbally and in written form so as to be scaffolded to help students learn the pattern of presentation. To help students reason addition and subtraction within 20, use a similar approach to that within 10 where students are manipulating concrete objects first and then using pictures before writing abstract equations. The example below shows a number line displaying $8 + 12 = 20$ and $20 - 12 = 8$.

Use multiple representations to show the interrelationship of addition and subtraction as well as properties of addition. As properties are learned, such as commutative, the number of facts to be memorized is reduced. For example, using an informal triangle strategy (Bird, 2009), it can be surmised that $6 + 2 = 8$ and $2 + 6 = 8$.

Additionally, to show the interrelationship it can be shown that 17 − 8 = 9 and 17 − 9 = 8.

Build verbal understandings of equations and practice them to help connect the meanings of number sentences to verbal sentences. See Chapters 8 and 9 for specific details.

In addition to the commutative property, the associative property can be shown on a number line. The example below shows 4 + 6 + 5 = 15. A student can redo this problem to show 4 + 5 + 6 also equals 15. Thus (4 + 6) + 5 = 4 + (5 + 6).

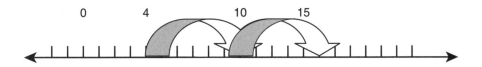

Learning associative and commutative properties to 10 will help later when regrouping numbers in multiple-digit computation. For example, when decomposing the above 4 + 6 + 5 = 15, a student can be shown (4 + 6) + 5 = 4 + (6 + 5) or 10 + 5 = 15. Learning relationships through different properties should reduce the number of facts to be memorized.

Even missing addends can be used with both the number line and the triangle strategy. Take for example the triangles shown earlier. Instead of having the students fill in each of the three corners of the triangle, have them premade with one containing a box instead of a number. Explain to the students that each box represents an unknown number. Ask them to determine the answer and work through the problems aloud. Assess not just their answer but their reasoning.

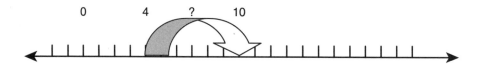

To develop fluency, first have students build groups of 10 such as 13 – 4 is the same as 13 – 3 – 1 and 7 + 5 is the same 7 + 3 + 2. Once 10s are mastered, focus on maximum minuends and sums of 20. Focusing on groups up to 10 and then multiple 10s ties to the need for place value, which is helpful with more complex computational problems. See Chapter 5 for more information.

To increase fluency, practice should occur using multiple methods, from the typical written exercises to verbal rehearsal in pairs using call or flash cards to quick paper quizzes and "I have/who has" cards, there are many ways to help students memorize their facts. Involve parents in this process as well by giving them objectives, methods, and time allotment.

16
I have 16. Who has 5 more than 8?

13
I have 13. Who has 3 less than 7?

Second Grade

With most of the expectations of addition and subtraction mastery occurring in the first grade, second grade becomes an extension of first. Word problems, missing addends, and maximum sums and addends of 100 are now the expectation. For word problems, present multiple verbs to show addition and subtraction both verbally and in word problems, just as in first grade. The difference for second grade is the complexity of the higher value of numbers and increased number of steps.

To extend the understanding of addition and subtraction comes the entrance of rectangular arrays, which represents the beginning of teaching multiples (i.e., skip counting). The expectation is set at 5 rows by 5 columns for a maximum of multiples of 5.

For example: 3 rows of 4 = 12

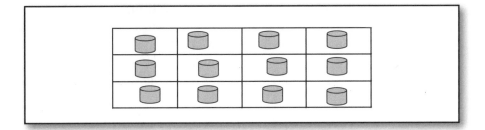

Another extension of addition and subtraction is measurement. Using a number line model, students can walk on a masking tape number line spaced per their feet to describe the measurement. Partial steps may even be used to describe fractional answers such as $3\frac{1}{2}$ steps.

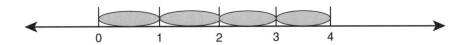

Memory

An absolute expectation of second-grade math is that "by end of Grade 2, know from memory all sums of two one-digit numbers" (CCSS, p. 19). Memory continues to be stressed in the new standards. Practice addition and subtraction facts until automatic. While many programs use a written practice format, either on the computer or on worksheets, it is important to use multiple formats, both verbal and written, so that students practice hearing and saying their facts as well as writing them.

> "Why did we only practice writing our facts, when we spend so much of our time now doing them in our heads?"
>
> —Comment from a future teacher, now fourth-grade student

Third Grade

The difference between the second-grade and third-grade expectation is the use of a letter variable in more complex word problems. Rephrase questions to include an unknown quantity. Since multiplication and division are still developing, problems should include lower numbers to ease calculation. A second-grade problem may read as follows: Suzy spent $8 for a movie ticket and $4 for popcorn. How much did she spend? This third grade standard is this: Suzy spent $8 on a movie ticket and an unknown amount b for popcorn. She spent $12 total. How much did she spend on popcorn?

Lastly, use a 100s grid to show patterns of addition and subtraction that will prepare multiplication and division. Each set of multiples shows a pattern. For example, the multiples of 8 are highlighted below.

0	1	2	3	4	5	6	7	8	9
10	11	12	13	14	15	16	17	18	19
20	21	22	23	24	25	26	27	28	29
30	31	32	33	34	35	36	37	38	39
40	41	42	43	44	45	46	47	48	49
50	51	52	53	54	55	56	57	58	59
60	61	62	63	64	65	66	67	68	69
70	71	72	73	74	75	76	77	78	79
80	81	82	83	84	85	86	87	88	89
90	91	92	93	94	95	96	97	98	99

Interventions for Students Struggling With Addition and Subtraction

Before intervening with addition and subtraction, start with counting. Strategic counting is a valid method, albeit slow, to performing addition and subtraction. For basic addition and subtraction, use several practice methods, one addend at a time. Start with addition of 0. Once students show mastery of adding 0, work on adding 1 to another addend. Then go to adding 2, and so on. Flash cards, practice sheets, and verbal methods should be used in a manner so that students are not practicing incorrectly. For example, if a student misses six flash cards in a set, teach only one card and then go back through the entire set with that one card in it. Then, teach another card and go back through the entire set with the two previously missed cards in it. Continue this pattern until the student can go through the set entirely without error.

Use of Apps

Many technology tools are available that support learning to count. One recently exciting tool is the Apple iPod or iPad (see Table 4.4). While each of these may be engaging to children, the use of iPads is limited to practice. At this point, very few apps include instructional components, such as an avatar actually modeling what to do and verbalizing reasoning. Another weakness is that too many apps that were reviewed overuse counting as a means for addition and subtraction. Use counting apps expeditiously until the child is able to use

Table 4.4   Sample Apps for Use in an iPod or iPad

Sample Counting Apps for Use in an iPod or iPad		
Application	*Usefulness*	*Cautions*
Toddler Counting by iTot Apps, LLC, in 2010 ($0.99)	Student is supposed to count the objects shown on the screen by touching them.	May be too youthful and must be used expeditiously to teach counting. Move quickly to cardinality.
Counting by Henk Dawson and Dave Peterson in 2011 ($0.99)	Numbers are presented by showing both numerals and counting circles in a 3×3 frame.	Designed for 3- to 6-year-olds. Combines numerals and number counting simultaneously.
Number Monster lite HD Counting by Creativeright Games in 2011 (free)	Interactive counting games with learning and challenge modes.	More fun than instructive but a reasonable and entertaining app.
Butterfly Math Addition by Pyzia, LLC, in 2011 (free)	Counting numbers of familiar and well-illustrated items.	Very interactive but is much more of an activity game that reinforces counting from 1 more than cardinality and addition.
Sample Number Identification App for Use in an iPod or iPad		
Application	*Usefulness*	*Cautions*
Animals Counting Writing Game HD by BrainCounts ($1.99)	Numerals and counting objects (animals) are presented. Students are to write the number in word form in a space provided.	Formation of letters to make words is not monitored. Be certain to teach letter formation before and during this app.

(Continued)

Table 4.4 (Continued)

Sample Addition and Subtraction Apps for Use in an iPod or iPad		
Application	*Usefulness*	*Cautions*
MathBoard by Palasoftware, Inc., in 2010–2011 ($4.99)	Covers all four operations including multiple-digit problems. You can choose an operation in which to focus and complete problems in the expandable writable work area.	Still uses a multiple-choice format, despite the excellent work space. Reviewing the student's work, however, allows you to grade the work more precisely.
Math Evolve by Zephyr Games in 2011 ($0.99)	Covers all four operations in an engaging story format.	It may be more engaging than educational. Shooting things is not for everyone.
Math Fact Master by TicTapTech, LLC, in 2011 ($0.99)	Covers all four operations and provides an analysis of student work per addend or factor.	Flash card format with keypad answer format. Good idea but will slow down fluency measures.
Arithmemouse by Tinman Learning (free)	Covers all four operations. Addition and subtraction are free, but there is a cost to upgrade for multiplication and division.	Some may have difficulty navigating the characters even if the answers are correct.
Tiny Chicken Learns Math by TapToLearn Software (free for a limited time)	Covers all four operations, with different levels of difficulty for all ages.	Has a timer, so students must calculate mentally.

Note: No auditory practice apps reviewed.

cardinality in order to prepare for addition and subtraction. Per the addition and subtraction apps, none reviewed emphasized properties, such as associative and identity, that would reduce the load needed for memorization.

Summary

Through a complex use of concrete and visual representations, students can learn numbers, counting, and beginning operational skills. Vertically aligning approaches will help students see the progressions from one grade level to the next. As students develop these principles, however, numbers will grow large quickly. Introduce place value around base 10 to help make sense of the pattern of multiple-digit numbers and the consistency of computational principles with different number values.

References

Bird, R. (2009). *Overcoming difficulties with number.* Thousand Oaks, CA: Sage.

Common Core State Standards for Mathematics. (n.d.). Retrieved June 1, 2011, from the Council of Chief State School Officers and the National Governors Association website: http://corestandards.org/assets/CCSSI_Math%20Standards.pdf

Geary, D. C., Hoard, M. K., Nugent, L., & Byrd-Craven, J. (2007). Strategy use, long-term memory, and working memory capacity. In D. B. Berch & M. M. M. Mazzocco (Eds.), *Why is math so hard for some children? The nature and origins of mathematical learning difficulties and disabilities.* Baltimore: Brookes.

Gersten, R., Clarke, B., Haymond, K., & Jordan, N. (2011). *Screening for mathematics difficulties in K–3 students* (2nd ed.). Portsmouth, NH: RMC Research Corporation, Center on Instruction.

Goldman, S. R., Pellegrino, J. W., & Mertz, D. L. (1988). Extended practice of basic addition facts: Strategy changes in learning-disabled students. *Cognition and Instruction, 5*(3), 223–265.

Hartmann, J. (n.d.). *Songs for teaching.* Retrieved July 30, 2011, from http://www.songsforteaching.com/jackhartmann/counting1to20.htm

Hasselbring, T. S., Goin, L., & Bransford, J. D. (1988). Developing math automaticity in learning handicapped children: The role of computerized drill and practice. *Focus on Exceptional Children, 20,* 1–7.

Krasa, N., & Shunkwiler, S. (2009). *Number sense and number nonsense: Understanding the challenges of learning math.* Baltimore: Brookes.

Laski, R. S., & Siegler, R. S. (2007). Is 27 a big number? Correlational and causal connections among numerical categorization, number line estimation, and numerical magnitude comparison. *Child Development, 78*(6), 1723–1743.

Olson, J. (2008). *Letters and numbers for me.* Gaithersburg, MD: Handwriting Without Tears.

Riccomini, P. J., & Witzel, B. S. (2010). *RTI in mathematics.* Thousand Oaks, CA: Corwin.

Siegler, R., Carpenter, T., Fennell, F., Geary, D., Lewis, J., Okamoto, Y., Thompson, L., & Wray, J. (2010). *Developing effective fractions instruction for kindergarten through 8th grade: A practice guide* (NCEE #2010-4039). Washington, DC: National Center for Education Evaluation and Regional Assistance, Institute of Education Sciences, U.S. Department of Education.

5

Building Computation Systems Through Place Value

Evaluating the many procedures taught to our students reveals a series of tricks that lack number sense. It's time to put reasoning and strategy back into mathematics instruction.

Bradley S. Witzel

Why do we compute mathematics from right to left in elementary mathematics but then support a left-to-right format thereafter? Why do we tell our students that you can't take 9 from 7 in a subtraction problem two years before they learn about negatives? It might be that our standard algorithms are developed to be math tricks that satisfy a single grade-level set of standards rather than designed from math logic and reasoning that progress through math skills and grade level. It may also be that we feel we need tricks to "get by" because our students live in a culture and language where mathematics is undervalued and concepts like number and place value are often misunderstood. No matter the cause, mathematics procedures should be based on logical reasoning supported by mathematical principles.

Key aspects of the chapter:

1. Place value is an essential skill in mathematics development.

2. Teach the language of place value explicitly.

3. Use concrete and visual representations to show how place value is used with magnitude comparisons and computation.

4. Knowledge of place value within operations can set the stage for computation of rational numbers.

The Place Value Imperative

A focus on place value and the base-10 system is necessary for students to understand numbers, communicate about mathematics, and compute accurately with reason. In preparing for early numeracy assessments, understanding place value is not always directly assessed; however, knowledge of place value pervades much of mathematics. Gersten, Clarke, Haymond, and Jordan (2011) stated, "While a test may not measure mental calculation and place value directly, measures of magnitude comparison indicate likely performance in those areas" (p. 6). Sharma (1993) set the stage for place value instruction when he showed that "any concept dependent on number is dependent on place value" (p. 2). Understanding place value benefits computation of multiple-digit whole numbers, decimals, and scientific notation. In fact, if mathematics procedures of whole numbers are based on concepts of place value, then students can scaffold those procedures further to such concepts as fractions and polynomials. However, this requires a focus on long-term growth rather than single-grade expectations.

To help set up students for place value procedures, it is important to prepare them for groupings of expressions and help them understand number value as they count and identify numbers. Most U.S. students view multiple-digit numbers individually side by side. For example, a student may see 543 (five hundred forty-three) as a 5, then a 4, and then a 3 (Clements, 2004). Instead the student should see five 100s, four 10s, and three 1s. By way of comparison, in several other languages of higher-performing math countries, the position of a number is directly tied to the spoken representation. For example, 543 in English is "five hundred forty-three" but in Chinese is spoken as "five hundreds four tens and three" (Uy, 2003). It should be noted that while other nations use place value consistently within their language, in the United States the use of place value in mathematics computation is restricted to mature learners. We need to teach place value understanding to students earlier.

Take a look at what happens when learners mature in their thinking. Most adults, teachers included, may have memorized and practiced the right-to-left algorithm for addition. However, when verbally asked questions like 43 + 25, they add the 10s place first and then the 1s (Thompson, 2009). Even when answering a subtraction question such as 52 – 17 they answer the 10s place first and then judge the 1s. Maybe it is that more adults understand integers, which are usually taught late in U.S. education. Maybe it is that their operational facility is good, which allows for estimation knowing that the answer must be below 40. Either way, it enables a left-to-right math process orientation, something practiced in secondary mathematics.

Place value requires an understanding that has implications for developing number sense and understanding when using algorithms and representations, standard and alternative, with whole number arithmetic (Cawley, Parmar, Lucas-Fusco, Kilian, & Foley, 2007). The *standard algorithm* is a term used frequently in the Common Core State Standards (CCSS). All three of the examples below represent standard algorithms. Approach A requires students to predetermine if a single subtraction step might result in a negative number, and then the student steals from the higher place value to re-create the problem to have no negatives. Approach B first involves expanding both the minuend and the subtrahend by 10s and 1s. Then, similar to Approach A, this approach requires a review of the two subtraction problems, separated by place value, and stealing from the higher place value to avoid any negative answer. Then, the student answers the highest place value first before moving on to the next place value. The final answer is the addition of each of the subtraction problems. The main difference between A and B is the expansion, which helps teach place value and the approach from left to right. Approach C is used less often and requires more knowledge of the number line. Like Approach B, this approach involves expanding the notation of the subtrahend and minuend based on place value. Next, students solve each place value operation and allow negatives for answers. The final answer is based on the operation of the answers. Unlike the other approaches, Approach C helps teach place value and is used with integers. There are few regroupings using this approach.

A. Work from right to left and exchange if a negative might have to be negotiated	B. Expand the place value to ease computation organization and compute afterward	C. Expand based on place value and compute from left to right accepting negatives
^{4}**52**^{12} $-\ 17$ 35	$40 + 12$ $-\ 10 - 7$ $+\ 30 + 5 = 35$	$50 + 2$ $-\ 10 - 7$ $+\ 40 - 5 = 35$

To show the extension of each of these to more complex problems, review subtraction with fractions. Expanded notation prepares students to see the differences of parts of numbers, even whole to fraction or whole to decimal.

A. Work from right to left and exchange if a negative might have to be negotiated	B. Expand the place value to ease computation organization and compute afterward	C. Expand based on place value and compute from left to right accepting negatives
^{3}**4**$^1/_4$$^{5/4}$ $-\ 1\,^3/_4$ $2\,^2/_4$	$+\ 3 + \,^5/_4$ $-\ 1 - \,^3/_4$ $2 + \,^2/_4$	$-\ 4 + \,^1/_4$ $-\ 1 - \,^3/_4$ $3 - \,^2/_4$

Kindergarten Preparation

"Numeral recognition is notoriously difficult in English compared to other languages. Some researchers suggest this may be a factor impeding the speed with which Americans learn mathematics" (Gersten, Clarke, Haymond, & Jordan, 2011, p. 8).

To prepare students for understanding place value, much can be done at home. The first is to reteach counting and number identification. Numbers in English are written in a left-to-right format where the leftmost number signifies the largest value, called place value. In a base-10 system, each successive place value varies by a multiple of 10. While written numbers are recorded in a fairly simple pattern, they are verbally presented in a more confusing manner. For the single digits, each has a name. However, when they are presented in a different number position, how the number is named changes. For example, 1 as a single digit is just that, "one." In the teens, 2 is not directly identified verbally but may instead be linked to the 1 in the 10s place in the number 12. In fact, the teens are confusing in that their verbal presentation is reversed from other two-digit numbers. This can cause confusion to early learners and those learning English. "Forty-one" and "fourteen" sound similar but represent different numbers. Per place value, this can cause confusion when learning about number position and value. Thus, even if students come to school being able to count, the counting numbers that many students chant may have little to do with value. It may be that non-English speakers have an advantage when it comes to place value. Many foreign countries whose students score the highest on international tests use single-digit number names and place value position when naming numbers. When they identify numbers, their place value language names the number of 10s and 1s. For example, 12 is referred to as "one 10, two 1s." See Table 5.1 for more examples. This format of numbers can be taught to young children along with more generic English spoken numbers.

Table 5.1 Number Identification Using Single-Digit Number Names and Place Value Position

0 zero	1 one	2 two	3 three	4 four	5 five	6 six	7 seven	8 eight	9 nine
10 one 10, zero 1s	11 one 10, one 1	12 one 10, two 1s	13 one 10, three 1s	14 one 10, four 1s	15 one 10, five 1s	16 one 10, six 1s	17 one 10, seven 1s	18 one 10, eight 1s	19 one 10, nine 1s
20 two 10s, zero 1s	21 two 10s, one 1	22 two 10s, two 1s	23 two 10s, three 1s	24 two 10s, four 1s	25 two 10s, five 1s	26 two 10s, six 1s	27 two 10s, seven 1s	28 two 10s, eight 1s	29 two 10s, nine 1s

"Reading the morning announcement with my daughter at preschool, she read, 'Good morning! Today's date is August two 10s, five 1s.' When the teacher turned to me with a confused look on her face, I explained that my daughter is bilingual. She speaks English and math."

—Father of a prepared math student

Along with speaking in place value, prepare children to think in place value and groupings. Teach children to differentiate objects based on easy-to-see attributes such as colors of blocks. Once children understand how to identify blocks based on the attribute, then they can group several objects based on that attribute. For example, "I have two red blocks, one blue block, and four more red blocks." Ask the children to describe the blocks. Teach each child to group by color to conclude "one blue block and six red blocks." This will help transition children to place value of whole numbers: "I have two 10s and three 2s and one more 10. Summarize what I have." This can transition to money using different bases: "I have two quarters, four pennies, one nickel, and five more pennies. Summarize what I have." Eventually this practice can transition to algebraic expressions: "I have $3x + 7y - 1x + 4$. Summarize what I have."

Materials

Use items that visually display base 10 to teach and show the value of numbers presented in different positions within a number. Base-10 blocks or student-created items that can show base 10 are easy to use when modeling or having students manipulate. Figure 5.1

Figure 5.1

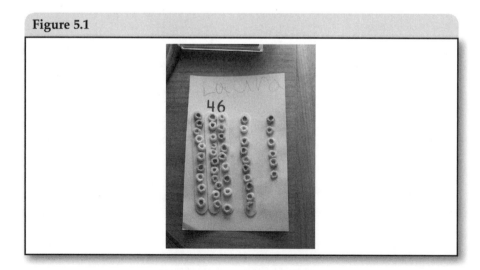

shows cereal glued to tongue depressors and paper that represents the 10s and 1s (place value) of a number.

CCSS

The developers of the CCSS (National Governors Association and Council of Chief State School Officers) took place value seriously. In the CCSS it is stated, "These Standards endeavor to follow such a design, not only by stressing conceptual understanding of key ideas, but also by continually returning to organizing principles such as place value or the properties of operations to structure those ideas" (p. 4). Thus, throughout the math standards, place value is a focus on learning numbers and computation. Table 5.2 shows place value standard progressions through early grade levels.

While it is not our intention to write an entire textbook series here, we hope that the many sample activities in this chapter show the relevance of an increased emphasis on place value throughout early childhood and elementary curricula. Using the information in this chapter in conjunction with the details specific to other areas of early numeracy in preceding chapters, we hope that it is obvious that place value knowledge is useful within the progressions of learning.

Kindergarten

As an early precursor skill to place value, using counting and cardinality skills, children should be able to compare two sets of objects using terms such as *greater than*, *less than*, and *equal to*. Within this development, teach groupings of 10 using bundles or cups of objects. The place value objective is that children should learn to identify one 10 and five 1s as larger than one 10 and four 1s. Two possible strategies that the child may use to solve this are grouping and counting-on. If the numbers are 10 or larger, then place value should be incorporated in the strategy. By visually or physically grouping the representations, the child may use cardinality to see that the representation on the left is larger than the one on the right. However, the child may not immediately determine the exact magnitude of each representation or the exact difference between each representation's magnitude and the other's. While the comparison is more efficient, many children may be compelled to count. If counting-on is used, the child should start by comparing each representation's 10 before proceeding to count on to determine that the left is 15 and the right is 14, making the left greater than the right.

Table 5.2 Place Value Standard Progressions Through Early Grade Levels

Number Sense Component	Kindergarten	First Grade	Second Grade	Third Grade
Magnitude Comparisons (place value)	K.CC.6. Identify whether the number of objects in one group is greater than, less than, or equal to the number of objects in another group, e.g., by using matching and counting strategies. K.CC.7. Compare two numbers between 1 and 10 presented as written numerals. K.NBT.1. Compose and decompose numbers from 11 to 19 into ten ones and some further ones, e.g., by using objects or drawings, and record each composition or decomposition by a drawing or	Number and Operations in Base Ten 1. NBT **Understand place value.** 2. Understand that the two digits of a two-digit number represent amounts of tens and ones. Understand the following as special cases: a. 10 can be thought of as a bundle of ten ones—called a "ten." b. The numbers from 11 to 19 are composed of a ten and one, two, three, four, five, six, seven, eight, or nine ones. c. The numbers 10, 20, 30, 40, 50, 60, 70, 80, 90 refer to one, two, three, four, five, six, seven, eight, or nine tens (and 0 ones). 3. Compare two two-digit numbers based on meanings of the tens and ones digits, recording the results of comparisons with the symbols >, =, and <. **Use place value understanding and properties of operations to add and subtract.**	Number and Operations in Base Ten 2.NBT **Understand place value.** 1. Understand that the three digits of a three-digit number represent amounts of hundreds, tens, and ones; e.g., 706 equals 7 hundreds, 0 tens, and 6 ones. Understand the following as special cases: a. 100 can be thought of as a bundle of ten tens—called a "hundred." b. The numbers 100, 200, 300, 400, 500, 600, 700, 800, 900 refer to one, two, three, four, five, six, seven, eight, or nine hundreds (and 0 tens and 0 ones). 3. Read and write numbers to 1,000 using base-ten numerals, number names, and expanded form. 4. Compare two three-digit numbers based on meanings of the hundreds, tens, and ones digits, using >, =, and < symbols to record the results of comparisons. **Use place value understanding and properties of operations to add and subtract.**	Number and Operations in Base Ten 3.NBT **Use place value understanding and properties of operations to perform multi-digit arithmetic.** 1. Use place value understanding to round whole numbers to the nearest 10 or 100. 2. Fluently add and subtract within 1,000 using strategies and algorithms based on place value, properties of operations, and/ or the relationship between addition and subtraction.

equation (such as 18 = 10 + 8); understand that these numbers are composed of ten ones and one, two, three, four, five, six, seven, eight, or nine ones.	1.NBT.4. Add within 100, including adding a two-digit number and a one-digit number, and adding a two-digit number and a multiple of 10, using concrete models or drawings and strategies based on place value, properties of operations, and/or the relationship between addition and subtraction; relate the strategy to a written method and explain the reasoning used. Understand that in adding two-digit numbers, one adds tens and tens, ones and ones; and sometimes it is necessary to compose a ten. 1.NBT.5. Given a two-digit number, mentally find 10 more or 10 less than the number, without having to count; explain the reasoning used. 1.NBT.6. Subtract multiples of 10 in the range 10–90 from multiples of 10 in the range 10–90 (positive or zero differences), using concrete models or drawings and strategies based on place value, properties of operations, and/or the relationship between addition and subtraction; relate the strategy to a written method and explain the reasoning used.	3. Multiply one-digit whole numbers by multiples of 10 in the range 10–90 (e.g., 9 × 80, 5 × 60) using strategies based on place value and properties of operations. 5. Fluently add and subtract within 100 using strategies based on place value, properties of operations, and/or the relationship between addition and subtraction. 6. Add up to four two-digit numbers using strategies based on place value and properties of operations. 7. Add and subtract within 1000, using concrete models or drawings and strategies based on place value, properties of operations, and/or the relationship between addition and subtraction; relate the strategy to a written method. Understand that in adding or subtracting three digit numbers, one adds or subtracts hundreds and hundreds, tens and tens, ones and ones; and sometimes it is necessary to compose or decompose tens or hundreds. 8. Mentally add 10 or 100 to a given number 100–900, and mentally subtract 10 or 100 from a given number 100–900. 9. Explain why addition and subtraction strategies work, using place value and the properties of operations.

Source: Standards found at http://www.corestandards.org/assets/CCSSI_Math%20Standards.pdf

In this illustration, a child lays down a picture of Greater Gator between two place value block representations to show that 15 is greater than 14. However, it is not enough that children are accurate in their magnitude comparisons. They must be able to reason abstractly using an understanding of place value. Thus, in the example above, the student should be able to explain that the number of 10s is equal between the two numbers but the greater number has one more 1 than the other. That is why 15 is greater than 14.

Decomposition of Place Value

Children must be able to explain how numbers, especially those in the teens, are composed of numbers of digits in respective place values. Have children decompose numbers such as 15 into one 10 plus five 1s. Decomposition of the teens beyond the unexplainable 11 and 12 but also the reverse-ordered 13 through 19 teaches students the meaning of number labels per number position and allows for a more even match from written number to verbal presentation. Use matching games such as "see and says" to help students practice. In a "see and says" game, students work in pairs to decipher place value of a number. The first student picks up a card and reads, "One hundred forty-six." The second student then must write down "146" and say, "One 100, four 10s, six 1s." Practicing place value orally not only aids memory but also helps when working with word problems.

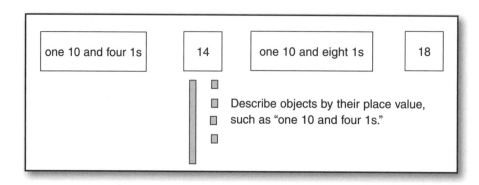

First Grade

By first grade, children should extend their use of place value language to consistently translate counting from "eleven, twelve, thirteen," and so on to "one 10, one 1; one 10, two 1s; one 10, three 1s" up through "one 100, zero 10s, zero 1s." Thus, children should see that "one 10, three 1s" is the same as "thirteen 1s." Physical props to help with the translation and development are accurately sized proportional base-10 objects that show 10s and teach the appropriate language.

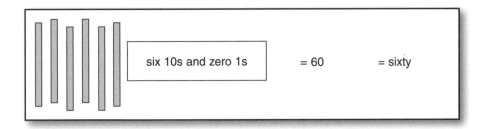

Teach progressions of the kindergarten magnitude comparison by increasing the values of the numbers to larger two-digit numbers using place value language. The student should be able to verbally conclude, "Three 10s and four 1s is greater than two 10s and seven 1s because three 10s is greater than two 10s." To form a baseline for subtraction, have students reasonably compare 10s and 1s and even ask for precision in their reasoning. A visual grouping comparison would be "Three 10s is one 10 more than two 10s, but four 1s is three less than seven 1s. Thus, there is a difference of 10 − 3 or 7."

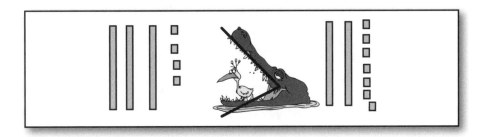

Addition and Subtraction Grow Larger

Teaching multiple-digit addition and subtraction should be based on place value understanding using properties of addition as well as previously introduced concrete and pictorial models. In the first grade, students are expected to perform two-digit and two- by one-digit addition and subtraction using previously gained number sense including magnitude of number and place value.

The use of standard algorithms across grades and districts helps students build from one mathematics skill to the next. A standard algorithm based on place value knowledge is through decomposition. The example shows addition of 26 + 18 through the concrete to representational to abstract sequence of instruction using the decomposition standard algorithm. Matching the concrete materials to the abstract equation helps when teaching students to reason through the algorithm. After setting up the concrete materials, ask if the two numbers 26 and 18 are going in the same or opposite directions on a number line. Relating addition and subtraction allows students to reason through the directionality of computation. This same approach will also be helpful when working in integer computation. In this example, since the two numbers both go in the same direction, the answer is found by counting on. The expanded notation and a place value approach to computation allows students to reason sets of 10s and 1s for the final product.

Concrete	Pictorial	Abstract
+ +	+ +	+ 20 + 6
+ +	+ +	+ 10 + 8
+ +	+ +	+ 30 + 14
= +	= +	= + 44

For subtraction, similar to addition, similar reasoning should prevail. Multiple-digit subtraction understanding and operation should be based on understanding of number sense. In the example below, the student is presented with 60 – 20 or "What is the difference between six 10s and two 10s?" To perform this concretely, set up a concrete equivalent of this equation. Lay down a positive sign and six 10s and a subtraction sign and two 10s. The student should be asked about direction on a number line: "Are these going in the same or opposite direction on a number line?" To solve a subtraction problem where you have a minuend and a subtrahend, you create pairs of 10s that equal zero, such that 10 – 10 = 0. In this example, take two 10s from each minuend and subtrahend. The answer is four 10s.

Concrete	Pictorial	Abstract
+	+	+ 60
–	–	– 20
+	+	+ 40

Second Grade

By second grade, students are decomposing three-digit numbers into 100s, 10s, and 1s using a similar approach to place value language as what was presented in earlier grades. Show groupings and exchanges of 1s to make 10s, 10s to make 100s, and even 1s to make 100s, although the latter is more cumbersome and time consuming. Using games such as "Race to 100," students create exchanges to show equality across place value language. Using this game format, two students work together to continuously increase the value on their board according to each roll of the dice. Thus, if the students already have 28 represented and they roll a 7 with their dice, they will lay down seven more 1s. They will then say, "Two 10s and fifteen 1s." Once the group says this interpretation, they exchange ten 1s for one 10 and say, "Is the same as three 10s and five 1s." This exchange continues until the group gets over 100. The exchange of 1s, 10s, and 100s and verbal interpretation helps students understand the exchanges and the expanded form of each number.

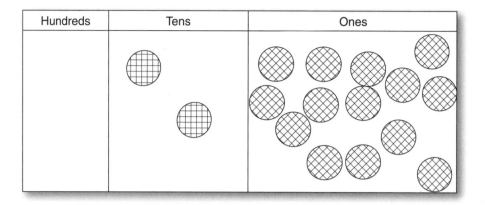

Hundreds	Tens	Ones

Once understood, expand the number system into thousands.

Figure 5.2

Magnitude of number continues in second grade by comparing 100s to support the place value language. If physical manipulations, such as Greater Gators, are used, then we have three extra suggestions that not only help students who have a weaker background but also prepare students for more advanced understandings.

1. Students who struggle with the concept should represent each number concretely and pictorially. Provide examples using bundled sticks or interlocking cubes to help show the magnitude of place value concepts. Use corresponding pictures of the concrete manipulative to provide an alternative to abstract notation.

2. As students use the concrete or pictorial aid, have them say aloud the numbers that they are comparing to help express the abstract number. Students should learn to compare magnitudes verbally, thus preparing them for automaticity of number sense.

3. Teach students to identify each of the numbers on a number line as preparation for the use of integers. Far too often, students think in absolute value that –34 is greater than –9. Instead, this lesson can begin to show that *greater* and *less than* are connected with directionality and magnitude on a number line.

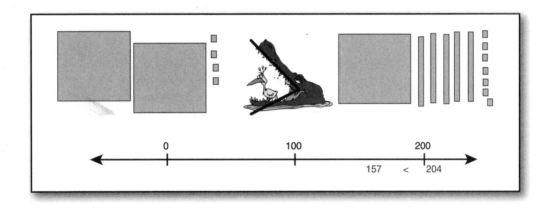

Progressions of Subtraction

Second-grade students should learn to use place value in their addition and subtraction up to at least 1,000. If the base strategy for addition and subtraction has been consistently using reasoning about the place value magnitude of number, then this demand should be a smooth transition. In the examples below, we show concrete, pictorial, and abstract methods for subtraction. The progressions that we show include strategies with regrouping and using integers, a method we describe in length earlier in this chapter.

While teaching place value understanding at the outset of number learning and formal schooling provides a strong start, this understanding must be used within computation so that the understanding is practiced. In this example of concrete to representational to abstract work, 33 – 18, the student must manipulate the 10s and 1s and then compute comparison subtraction as shown earlier before regrouping was required.

Concrete	Pictorial	Abstract
		+ 30 + 3
		– 10 – 8
		+ 20 + 13
		– 10 – 8
		+ 10 + 5 = 15

12	10 + 2	321	300 + 20 + 1
–8	–8	–186	–100 – 80 – 6
	2 + 2 = 4		

200 + 110 + 11
–100 – 80 – 6
100 + 30 + 5 = 135

$$\begin{array}{r} 1\ 3 \\ -\ 7 \\ \hline 6 \end{array}$$

$$\begin{array}{r} \overset{2}{\cancel{3}}\ \overset{\overset{1}{1}}{\cancel{2}}\ \overset{11}{\cancel{1}} \\ -\ 1\ 8\ 6 \\ \hline 1\ 3\ 5 \end{array}$$

An alternative for those who understand that numbers work on a line rather than on a ray may better understand using integers in their subtraction rather than regrouping.

$$321$$
$$\underline{-186}$$

$$300 + 20 + 1$$
$$\underline{-100 - 80 - 6}$$
$$200 - 60 - 5$$

$$140 \quad - 5 = 135$$

To show an example of subtraction using integers, see how this student sets up the problem from concrete to representational to abstract.

Concrete	Pictorial	Abstract
		+ 30 + 3
		− 10 − 8
		+ 20 − 5
		+ 20 − 5 = 15

Figure 5.3

Further Progressions to Upper Elementary

As students progress in grade level, their understandings and uses of place value should turn from conceptual and procedural to more automatic. For example, learning *3.NBT.3. Multiply one-digit whole numbers by multiples of 10 in the range 10–90 (e.g., 9 × 80, 5 × 60) using strategies based on place value and properties of operations*, students should think in terms of groups of 10 objects.

4 × 20 or four groups of two 10s = eight 10s = 80

30 × 5 or three 10s in each of five groups = fifteen 10s = 150

The same holds true for division. In fourth grade, students learning *4.NBT.1. Recognize that in a multi-digit whole number, a digit in one place represents ten times what it represents in the place to its right*, use place value in terms of number of groups of 10s that go into other groups.

600 ÷ 60 or sixty 10s ÷ six 10s = 10. Likewise, 60 × 10 is the same as 600.

For a glimpse at where these progressions develop, fifth grade calls for computation of rational numbers using strategies founded in place value.

5.NBT.7. Add, subtract, multiply, and divide decimals to hundredths, using concrete models or drawings and strategies based on place value, properties of operations, and/or the relationship between addition and subtraction; relate the strategy to a written method and explain the reasoning used.

The example below, 1.3 × 2.7, shares the place value language that extends students' understandings of computation. While some may falsely simplify this computation as "one point three times two point seven," it should be viewed as "one and three-tenths times two and seven-tenths." The latter elucidates the use of place value language and is explicitly used in this array form of multiplication.

Array for multiplying	1	.3
2	"One times two is two" 2	"Three-tenths times two is six-tenths" 0.6
.7	"One times seven-tenths is seven-tenths" 0.7	"Three-tenths times seven-tenths is twenty-one hundredths" 0.21

To complete the problem, the student adds the products: 2 + 0.6 + 0.7 + 0.21 = 3.51.

Intervention for Place Value

Understanding place value may be difficult for several students. Focus on concrete objects and verbal practice before applications. It may be that the child cannot make the connection between what is more commonly spoken and the place value language. In these cases, have children create bundles of 10 objects, such as toothpicks, popsicle sticks, or barrels of apples, before they use prepackaged base-10 products. Once the child can bundle the groups of 10, then the child will be better able to understand the use of base-10 blocks, which come already prepackaged as bundles of 10 and 100. Although these approaches to computation are the foundation for many of the algorithms that people have learned, they may appear very different. Because of this difference, some parents may resist the instruction. To help parents support their children, include instructions on how to use the language and compute differently and provide reasons why it is so very valuable to later learning, such as rational numbers. It may be most beneficial to provide video instruction. The consistent use of place value language with a more frequent connection to base-10 objects should help provide a stronger foundation for the child.

Apps

There are few applications for an iPad available that express math as a base-10 system of computation (see Table 5.3). It may be that the CCSS have not been reviewed as to their progressions. It is our hope that place value and base 10 will be more frequently used by students, teachers, and computer engineers.

Table 5.3   Sample Place Value App for Use in an iPod or iPad

Application	Usefulness	Cautions
RoboLearning: Math Word Problems 1 by David R. Fox in 2011 ($1.99)	Presents word problems on an illustrated robot. The program is inviting, and the problems are fairly straightforward.	Does not show how to solve problems, there are no visuals other than the robot's picture, and answers are presented in a multiple-choice format.

Conclusion

A strong understanding of math should start with a strong finish. Understanding not just counting but position and related magnitude is an important part of a student's development of math and number sense. The purpose of this chapter was to show the uses of place value across grade-level understanding within the framework of the CCSS. While the utility of place value aids in understanding of whole number operations and computation, it has been linked to understanding of rational numbers as well.

References

Cawley, J. F., Parmar, R. S., Lucas-Fusco, L. M., Kilian, J. D., & Foley, T. E. (2007). Place value and mathematics for students with mild disabilities: Data and suggested practices. *Learning Disabilities: A Contemporary Journal, 15*(1), 21–39.

Clements, D. H. (2004). Major themes and recommendations. In D. H. Clements, J. Sarama, & A. M. DiBiase (Eds.), *Engaging young children in mathematics: Standards for early childhood mathematics education.* (pp. 1–72). Mahwah, NJ: Lawrence Erlbaum Associates.

Common Core State Standards for Mathematics. (n.d.). Retrieved June 1, 2011, from the Council of Chief State School Officers and the National Governors Association website: http://corestandards.org/assets/ CCSSI_Math%20Standards.pdf

Gersten, R., Clarke, B., Haymond, K., & Jordan, N. (2011). *Screening for mathematics difficulties in K–3 students.* Portsmouth, NH: RMC Research Corporation, Center on Instruction.

Sharma, M. C. (1993). Place value concept: How children learn it and how to teach it. *Math Notebook, 10*(1&2), 1–23.

Thompson, I. (2009). Place value? *Mathematics Teaching, 215,* 4–5.

Uy, F. (2003). The Chinese numeration system and place value. *Teaching Children Mathematics, 9*(5), 43–47.

6

Multiplication and Division

Learning multiplication facts is a first step in proportional reasoning, "the capstone of elementary arithmetic and the gateway to higher mathematics" (Kilpatrick, Swafford, & Findell, 2001, p. 242). Proportional reasoning, in turn, is central to success in money management, chemistry, physics, economics, and all phenomena involving change.

Flowers & Rubenstein, 2010, p. 296

Classroom Instruction

Instructional strategies used in the classroom can either embrace or hinder the learning opportunities of students. Being an effective teacher begins with the right kind of thinking from the teacher. Sezer (2008) concluded that critical thinking can have positive effects on students' attitudes. In the past, teaching was driven solely by rote memorization through paper-and-pencil tasks. Students worked in workbooks, read textbooks, and practiced what they were never thoroughly taught. Today, instruction is leaning toward the problem-solving process. Sezer's study found that using problem-solving methods in instruction allowed students to monitor their own thinking, critique their own thinking, and contribute overall to group thinking skills. The Common Core State Standards (CCSS) address the need for problem solving throughout the mathematic domains. Students are taken to a deeper approach with understanding mathematics through questioning and explanation of tasks.

> One hallmark of mathematical understanding is the ability to justify, in a way appropriate to the student's mathematical maturity, *why* a particular mathematical statement is true or where a mathematical rule comes from. . . . The student who can explain the rule understands the mathematics. (CCSS, p. 4)

Gullatt (2008) addressed the fact that teachers need to move away from being "dispenser[s] of knowledge" and provide opportunities for student engagement and interactivity with the content. Table 6.1 provides a selection of possible ways of multiplicative instruction through problem solving.

Table 6.1 Multiplicative Problem Solving

Student Problem	Teacher's Role	Student Work	Desired Student Responses
Timmy has 4 boxes of crayons. Each box contains 9 crayons. How many crayons does Timmy have in all?	Provide tools to solve the problem. Be a facilitator. Teacher: *"What is the problem asking you to do—where will you begin to solve the problem, and why?"* During the problem-solving process: *"Why do you feel the chosen tool was the best? Could another tool work just as well?"* Conclusion of the lesson: *"Is there a way you can write this problem in a number sentence?"*	Chooses an appropriate tool to solve the problem. Reviews question and finds a place to start working. Begins working on the problem showing the solution through concrete tools and clear explanation.	*"I chose the cubes so I can count them easily."* *"I need to add because the problem wants to know how many in all."* *"I made 4 groups of 9 because each crayon box has 9 crayons and there are 4 boxes."* Student makes a connection to skip counting and repeated addition. Further thinking would lead to the algorithm of multiplication.

The CCSS highlight strategic use of tools to solve mathematical problems. Tools can be an assortment of concrete manipulatives, rulers, protractors, and paper-and-pencil availability (see Table 6.2).

Table 6.2   CCSS-Recommended Tools for Mathematics Problem Solving

Instructional Domain	Toolbox Tools
Counting & Cardinality	Number line, counting blocks, bears, Unifix cubes
Operations & Algebraic Thinking	100s chart, yarn
Number & Operations in Base 10	Base-10 blocks
Number & Operations: Fractions	Fraction squares
Measurement & Data	Measuring tape, rulers, balance scales, weights
Geometry	2D and 3D shapes, foldable shapes (nets)

Note: Several items should always remain in the toolbox to provide concrete support. Dry erase markers, dry erase boards, and counting blocks should remain accessible for every instructional domain.

Varol and Farran (2006) discussed the importance of providing the materials and classroom environment to let this type of learning occur. Having the right mathematical tools to use for manipulation in constructing new meaning is important for teachers to remember when setting up a classroom and all throughout instruction. In a study conducted by Park (2005) it was concluded that students who were actively engaged in the mathematics lesson had higher achievement than students not engaged in the lesson. Park's study emphasized that student learning styles and student ability (learning disability or language barriers) had no effect on the achievement in mathematics.

Multiplication Difficulties

Throughout education there are many myths and misunderstandings when it comes to multiplication understanding and mastery. Most educators feel that students who recite multiplication tables have complete understanding because they have the answer. The problem may be that the foundation and understanding of what multiplication truly is have not been mastered. The two-year longitudinal study conducted by Mulligan and Mitchelmore (1997) outlined numerous strategies for multiplication problems (see Table 6.3).

The foundation of number sense and one-to-one correspondence must be mastered before moving into repeated addition, skip counting, and finally multiplication practice. The stages of instruction need to

Table 6.3 Multiplicative Strategies

Strategy	Definition	Examples
Direct Counting	Concrete materials used to count and model the problem. Multiplicative structure not referenced.	☐ ☐ ☐ ☐
Rhythmic Counting	Counting follows the problem structure. Simultaneously with counting, a second count is kept of the number of groups.	1, 2, 3, 4, 5, 6 or 6, 5, 4, 3, 2
Skip Counting	Counting in multiples makes it easier to keep track of the number of groups.	2, 4, 6, 8 5, 10, 15, 20
Additive Calculation/ Repeated Addition	Calculations replace counting.	$3 + 3 = 6, 6 + 3 = 9$
Multiplicative Calculation	Calculations of known facts derive from known facts.	2 times 4 is 8 or $2 \times 4 = 2 + 2 + 2 + 2$
Commutative Law	Changing the order does not change the outcome.	$6 \times 3 = 3 \times 6$
Distributive Law	$a \times (b + c) = a \times b + a \times c$ or vice versa.	2 times 6 is $2 \times (3 + 3) = 2 \times 3 + 3 \times 2$

Source: Adapted from Mulligan and Mitchelmore (1997); Wong and Evans (2007).

follow the concrete to representational to abstract (CRA) model. The first stage of instruction is through concrete practice. The concrete stage sets the foundation of mathematical understanding using concrete manipulatives. Following the concrete stage is representational work. Students will use this time to illustrate their understanding, which moves beyond the concrete, hands-on manipulative stage, but are not quite ready for an abstract algorithm. In the abstract stage students are able to solve an algorithm without concrete tools or visual representations. Daft's (2010) work has encompassed a variety of techniques in moving along the CRA stages of multiplication development beginning with pattern recognition (see Table 6.4).

For the first steps of instruction through CRA, students should not be given time restraints. Wong and Evans (2007) affirmed that for students participating in a concrete stage, time constraints are not appropriate. However, once a student has moved into an abstract stage, time restrictions should be set to improve speed and recall of multiplicative facts. Gradually reducing time allotted for each fact in the abstract time is recommended.

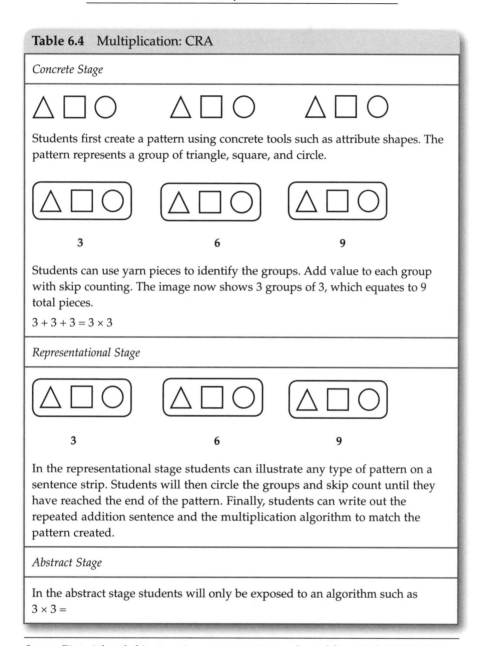

Table 6.4   Multiplication: CRA

Concrete Stage

Students first create a pattern using concrete tools such as attribute shapes. The pattern represents a group of triangle, square, and circle.

Students can use yarn pieces to identify the groups. Add value to each group with skip counting. The image now shows 3 groups of 3, which equates to 9 total pieces.

$3 + 3 + 3 = 3 \times 3$

Representational Stage

In the representational stage students can illustrate any type of pattern on a sentence strip. Students will then circle the groups and skip count until they have reached the end of the pattern. Finally, students can write out the repeated addition sentence and the multiplication algorithm to match the pattern created.

Abstract Stage

In the abstract stage students will only be exposed to an algorithm such as $3 \times 3 =$

Source: Pictorial and skip counting representations adapted from Daft (2010), *Moving Through Math: Repeating Patterns: Laying the Foundation for Elementary Mathematics, Lesson Plans for Teachers K–12,* www.marciadaft.com.

Common Core State Standards

The Common Core State Standards (CCSS) have been mapped to develop students' conceptual and procedural facility of multiplication and division through the use of multiple representations and stages of learning. See Table 6.5 for the CCSS grade-level progressions of multiplication and division development.

Table 6.5 Multiplication Progression

Kindergarten	First Grade	Second Grade	Third Grade
K.CC.1. Count to 100 by ones and by tens.	1.NBT.5. Given a two-digit number, mentally find 10 more or 10 less than the number, without having to count. Explain the reasoning used. 1.OA.3. Apply properties of operations as strategies to add and subtract. *Examples: If 8 + 3 = 11 is known, then 3 + 8 = 11 is also known. (Commutative property of addition). To add 2 + 6 + 4, the second two numbers can be added to make a ten, so 2 + 6 + 4 = 2 + 10 = 12. (Associative property of addition.)* 1.OA.8. Determine the unknown whole number in an addition or subtraction equation relating to three whole numbers. *For example, determine the unknown number that makes the equation true in*	2.NBT.2. Count within 1,000; skip-count by 5s, 10s, and 100s. 2.OA.1. Use addition and subtraction within 100 to solve one- and two-step word problems involving situations of adding to, taking from, putting together, taking apart, and comparing, with unknowns in all positions, e.g., by using drawings and equations with a symbol for the unknown number to represent the problem. 2.OA.4. Use addition to find the total number of objects arranged in rectangular arrays with up to 5 rows and up to 5 columns; write an equation to express the total as a sum of equal addends.	3.OA.1. Interpret products of whole numbers, e.g., interpret 5 × 7 as the total number of objects in 5 groups of 7 objects each. *For example, describe a context in which a total number of objects can be expressed as 5 × 7.* 3.OA.2. Interpret whole-number quotients of whole numbers, e.g., interpret 56 ÷ 8 as the number of objects in each share when 56 objects are partitioned equally into 8 shares, or as a number of shares when 56 objects are partitioned into equal shares of 8 objects each. *For example, describe a context in which a number of shares or a number of groups can be expressed as 56 ÷ 8.* 3.OA.3. Use multiplication and division within 100 to solve word problems in situations involving equal groups, arrays, and measurement quantities, e.g., by using drawings and equations with a symbol for the unknown number to represent the problem. 3.OA.4. Determine the unknown whole number in a multiplication or division equation relating three whole numbers. *For example, determine the unknown number that makes the equation true in each of the equations 8 × ? = 48, 5 = □ ÷ 3, 6 × 6 = ?.*

Kindergarten	First Grade	Second Grade	Third Grade
	each of the equations 8 + ? = 11, 5 = □ – 3, 6 + 6 = □.		**Understand properties of multiplication and the relationship between multiplication and division.** 3.OA.5. Apply properties of operations as strategies to multiply and divide. *Examples: If 6 × 4 = 24 is known, then 4 × 6 = 24 is also known. (Commutative property of multiplication.) 3 × 5 × 2 can be found by 3 × 5 = 15, then 15 × 2 = 30, or by 5 × 2 = 10, then 3 × 10 = 30. (Associative property of multiplication.) Knowing that 8 × 5 = 40 and 8 × 2 = 16, one can find 8 × 7 as 8 × (5 + 2) = (8 × 5) + (8 × 2) = 40 + 16 = 56. (Distributive property.)* 3.OA.6. Understand division as an unknown-factor problem. *For example, find 32 ÷ 8 by finding the number that makes 32 when multiplied by 8.* **Multiply and divide within 100.** 3.OA.7. Fluently multiply and divide within 100, using strategies such as the relationship between multiplication and division (e.g., knowing that 8 × 5 = 40, one knows 40 ÷ 5 = 8) or properties of operations. By the end of Grade 3, know from memory all products of two one-digit numbers.

Source: Standards found at http://www.corestandards.org/assets/CCSSI_Math%20Standards.pdf

Setting Multiplicative Foundation

K.CC.1. Count to 100 by ones and by tens.

Use a 100s chart to assist with counting by 1s and 10s. Have students place a transparent chip once they reach 10, 20, 30, 40, 50, 60, 70, 80, 90, and 100. Another alternative would be to laminate the 100s chart and have students circle the numbers. The visual aid of the 100s chart (see Figure 6.1) will help kindergarteners see the sequence of what number comes before and after.

Figure 6.1   100s Chart

1	2	3	4	5	6	7	8	9	10
11	12	13	14	15	16	17	18	19	20
21	22	23	24	25	26	27	28	29	30
31	32	33	34	35	36	37	38	39	40
41	42	43	44	45	46	47	48	49	50
51	52	53	54	55	56	57	58	59	60
61	62	63	64	65	66	67	68	69	70
71	72	73	74	75	76	77	78	79	80
81	82	83	84	85	86	87	88	89	90
91	92	93	94	95	96	97	98	99	100

1.NBT.5. Given a two-digit number, mentally find 10 more or 10 less than the number, without having to count. Explain the reasoning used.

The CCSS have outlined a distinct terminology for understanding place value (i.e., 13 is known as one 10 and three 1s). Students must understand this concept and transfer that knowledge to mentally find 10 more or 10 less with two-digit numbers. Using a 100s chart in a concrete and representational stage, students can practice identifying the pattern with adding or subtracting 10 from a given number.

2.NBT.2. Count within 1000; skip-count by 5s, 10s, and 100s.

By second grade, students can use the visual aid of a 100s chart to skip count by 5s and 10s. The most common skip counting in young children is 5, 10, 15, 20, and so on. However, students need exposure and practice with other numbers that can be skip counted by 5.

Example:

Beginning with a random number, count by 5s.

33, 38, 43, 48, 53, 58

Ask students if they notice a pattern within the numbers. They should see the alternating ones place from 3 to 8 and back to 3 each time. This pattern and skip-counting recognition is equally important to 5, 10, 15, and so on.

Moving Into Multiplication

2.OA.4. Use addition to find the total number of objects arranged in rectangular arrays with up to 5 rows and up to 5 columns; write an equation to express the total as a sum of equal addends.

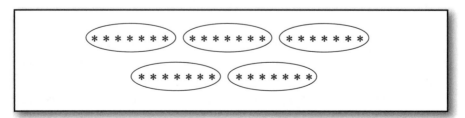

5 + 5 + 5 + 5 + 5 = 25 is shown as an array of 5 × 5

3.OA.1: Interpret products of whole numbers, e.g., interpret 5 × 7 as the total number of objects in 5 groups of 7 objects each. *For example, describe a context in which a total number of objects can be expressed as 5 × 7.*

Example:

5 groups of 7

Figure 6.2   The student shows all stages of understanding multiplication through manipulatives.

3.OA.2. Interpret whole-number quotients of whole numbers, e.g., interpret 56 ÷ 8 as the number of objects in each share when 56 objects are partitioned equally into 8 shares, or as a number of shares when 56 objects are partitioned into equal shares of 8 objects each. *For example, describe a context in which a number of shares or a number of groups can be expressed as 56 ÷ 8.*

Example:

Sally baked 56 cookies for her friends at school. She was planning to give each of her 8 friends an equal share. How many cookies would Sally give to each friend?

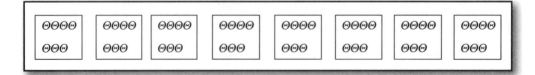

Likewise, develop students' problem solving using mathematics sentences and equations across grade levels. By third grade, students learn to find a missing multiplicand, 3, for the equation $\square \times 5 = 15$ or the multiplier, 5, for the equation $3 \times \square = 15$. See Table 6.6 for

Table 6.6 Solving for the Unknown

1.OA.8. Determine the unknown whole number in an addition or subtraction equation relating to three whole numbers. *For example, determine the unknown number that makes the equation true in each of the equations 8 + ? = 11, 5 = □ − 3, 6 + 6 = □.*	2.OA.1. Use addition and subtraction within 100 to solve one- and two-step word problems involving situations of adding to, taking from, putting together, taking apart, and comparing, with unknowns in all positions, e.g., by using drawings and equations with a symbol for the unknown number to represent the problem.	3.OA.4. Determine the unknown whole number in a multiplication or division equation relating three whole numbers. *For example, determine the unknown number that makes the equation true in each of the equations 8 × ? = 48, 5 = □ ÷ 3, 6 × 6 = ?.* 3.OA.6. Understand division as an unknown-factor problem. *For example, find 32 ÷ 8 by finding the number that makes 32 when multiplied by 8.*

First-grade students are expected to find the unknown whole number in a variety of equations. This sets the foundation for progression into second and third grade.

8 + ? = 11 5 = □ − 3 6 + 6 = □	8 + y = 11 5 = x − 3 6 + 6 = n	8 × ? = 48 5 = □ ÷ 3 6 × 6 = ?

Source: Standards found at http://www.corestandards.org/assets/CCSSI_Math%20Standards.pdf

the CCSS progressions for learning to solve equations using multiplication and division.

The Relationship Between Multiplication and Division

Upon transition into learning multiplication facts, students need to understand commutative and associative property. Understanding the commutative property decreases the amount of facts students will need to memorize by almost half. Commutative property applies to addition, subtraction, and multiplication facts. Associative property is also crucial for a strong understanding in addition, subtraction, and multiplication facts. Students need to go beyond knowing basic facts for recall, but also understand the ways facts can be manipulated to reach the same outcome. See Table 6.7 for information where properties are included in the CCSS.

Table 6.7   Properties of Operations

| 1.OA.3. Apply properties of operations as strategies to add and subtract. *Examples: If 8 + 3 = 11 is known, then 3 + 8 = 11 is also known. (Commutative property of addition.) To add 2 + 6 + 4, the second two numbers can be added to make a ten, so 2 + 6 + 4 = 2 + 10 = 12. (Associative property of addition.)* | 3.OA.5. Apply properties of operations as strategies to multiply and divide. *Examples: If 6 × 4 = 24 is known, then 4 × 6 = 24 is also known. (Commutative property of multiplication.) 3 × 5 × 2 can be found by 3 × 5 = 15, then 15 × 2 = 30, or by 5 × 2 = 10, then 3 × 10 = 30. (Associative property of multiplication.) Knowing that 8 × 5 = 40 and 8 × 2 = 16, one can find 8 × 7 as 8 × (5 + 2) = (8 × 5) + (8 × 2) = 40 + 16 = 56. (Distributive property.)* 3.OA.7. Fluently multiply and divide within 100, using strategies such as the relationship between multiplication and division (e.g., knowing that 8 × 5 = 40, one knows 40 ÷ 5 = 8) or properties of operations. By the end of Grade 3, know from memory all products of two one-digit numbers. |

Source: Standards found at http://www.corestandards.org/assets/CCSSI_Math%20 Standards.pdf

Moving Through Multiplication

There are three stages of finding multiplication proficiency: accuracy, fluency, and automaticity. As stated by Wong and Evans (2007), systematic practice of skills and knowledge to an automatic level of proficiency will allow students to retrieve facts from memory without conscious effort. Students who are unable to retrieve basic facts from memory will have a difficult time attending to more difficult and complex tasks.

Accuracy to Fluency

Accuracy of the skill is fundamental in continuing the learning progression of any mathematical concept. The first step is to establish students' level of proficiency. To first gain accuracy, many students will count objects. In a problem such as 7 × 2 or 7(2), the student may place seven groups of two objects. Teach the student to count by multiples (e.g., skip counting) from 2 to 14. Then, ask the student to repeat the problem and answer, "Seven times two is fourteen." Accuracy is a first step, but there are some roadblocks. As stated earlier, students with disabilities who seek accuracy overly rely on finger counting to reach their answer (Geary, 2004). While fingers are fantastic manipulative devices, they can also slow down a student when building fluency and automaticity later. Use fingers and concrete objects expeditiously. Once accurate, it is important to build to fact fluency and automaticity.

Intervention for Multiplication Fluency and Automaticity

"Quick retrieval of basic arithmetic facts is critical for success in mathematics. Yet research has found that many students with difficulties in mathematics are not fluent in such facts" (Gersten et al., 2009, p. 37). Once the foundation of multiplication accuracy is concrete, students must move from fluency and automaticity. For students who struggle in mathematics and require intervention, fluency is particularly difficult. Fluency, similar to word call accuracy in reading with smooth techniques, is to work through facts quickly. Table 6.8 lists several strategies for multiplication practice.

Table 6.8	Strategies for Multiplication Practice
Flashcards	Use flash cards to practice facts. Students can partner up. Student A flashes a card for five seconds to Student B. If Student B answers correctly, move to the next card. If the answer is incorrect, give the correct answer and move to the next card. This practice works well with the fluency to automaticity stage.
	Caution: Use flash cards sequentially growing as students demonstrate mastery. Presenting too much at once may adversely affect a student's working memory. With a third-grade student who evidenced difficulties with multiplication, the Tier 2 interventionist started with multiplication of 0s to 2s. For 2×6, the student said 10. The teacher responded 2 times 6 is 12. She then showed him using groups of blocks. Next, she asked him to repeat the question and answer $2 \times 6 = 12$ two times. Then she proceeded to place the flash card three deep in the stack of multiplication cards.
	She did not create a stack of wrong answers knowing that the student would likely struggle memorizing them all at once following the exercise.
Computer-Based Programs	Several computer-based programs have automatic feedback for students practicing facts. Some programs are as follows: • TransMath for Grades 5–10 • SRA Math Skillbuilder for Grades 1–8 • FASTT Math for Grades 2–5

(Continued)

Table 6.8 (Continued)

Math Folders	Using manila folders, masking tape, and page protectors, create math folders for each student. Tape the page protectors down the middle seam lying on the right-hand side, open side up. Place basic fact worksheets in the page protectors and provide students with dry erase markers and erasers. Set a timer and have students complete as many facts as possible in the set time. Have students score their own work using an answer key. On the left side of the manila folder provide a graph sheet so students can chart their growth each day.

The student may still rely on some visual representation; however, he or she has the foundation and understanding to solve the problem. Fluency will grow into automaticity, quick recall of facts, after repeated practice. Practice should consist of both written and oral/auditory practice. If practice is isolated to one form of cognition, then that is the only way you can ensure students are automatic. Design practice not only with written forms of fact practice but also with such auditory means as flash cards, partner sharing, and "I have/who has" exercises. This can be found by providing a timed pretest of multiplication facts. Proficiency is determined by the number of correct answers. A goal to set for most students is either 20 written multiplication problems per minute or 30 oral/auditory problems per minute.

Technology

Technology can be an important tool to learning multiplication and division and developing fluency. When students struggle with multiplication, it is a mistake to react by asking a calculator to complete the computation for a student. Rather than technology being used to supplant fluency, technology can be used to check accuracy and even develop fluency. Calculators are excellent devices for checking accuracy and an effective instructional device with students who have already mastered multiplication. But calculators are not the only mathematics technology that benefits students. See Table 6.9 for a list of apps that may help students practice multiplication and division.

Table 6.9 Sample Multiplication and Division Apps for Use in an iPod or iPad

Application	Usefulness	Cautions
Rocket Math by Dan Russell-Pinson in 2010 ($0.99)	All four operations with multiple-choice answers.	Written only and multiple choice limits the effects of the practice.

Application	Usefulness	Cautions
MathTappers: Multiples by Heavy Lifters Network, LLC, in 2010 (free)	Using array models and multiples, students can practice multiplicative reasoning. Can focus on multiplication in standard form or missing factors and can focus on one factor at a time.	Multiple-choice format is limiting and does not necessarily teach fluency. Still, it can be used as part of the learning process.
Times Tables by Rob Clarke in 2011 ($0.99)	Multiplication practice that can be configured for specific problem sets by factor.	More quiz-like in a multiple-choice format is limiting.
Multiplication Genius × 19 by Blue Onion Soft in 2011 (free for factors 2 through 5)	Displays the multiplication tables through 19, can be set by 9s, by 12s, and up to 19. Comes in both English and Korean.	Multiple-choice format in a quiz-type format.

Note: No auditory practice reviewed.

References

Common Core State Standards for Mathematics. (n.d.). Retrieved June 1, 2011, from the Council of Chief State School Officers and the National Governors Association website: http://corestandards.org/assets/CCSSI_Math%20Standards.pdf

Daft, M. (2010). *Repeating patterns: Laying the foundation for elementary mathematics.* Missarmira Productions.

Flowers, J. M., & Rubenstein, R. N. (2010). Multiplication fact fluency using doubles. *Mathematics Teaching in the Middle School, 16*(5), 296–301.

Geary, D. C. (2004). Mathematics and learning disabilities. *Journal of Learning Disabilities, 37,* 4–15.

Gersten, R., Beckmann, S., Clarke, B., Foegen, A., Marsh, L., Star, J. R., & Witzel, B. (2009). *Assisting students struggling with mathematics: Response to Intervention (RTI) for elementary and middle schools* (NCEE 2009-4060). Washington, DC: National Center for Education Evaluation and Regional Assistance, Institute of Education Sciences, U.S. Department of Education. Retrieved from http://ies.ed.gov/ncee/wwc/publications/practiceguides/

Gullatt, D. (2008, April/May). Enhancing student learning through arts integration: Implications for the profession. *The High School Journal,* 12–25.

Kilpatrick, J., Swafford, J., & Findell, B. (Eds.). (2001). *Adding it up: Helping children learn mathematics.* Washington, DC: National Research Council.

Mulligan, J. T., & Mitchelmore, M. C. (1997). Young children's intuitive models of multiplication and division. *Journal for Research in Mathematics Education, 28*(3), 309–331.

Park, S. (2005). Student engagement and classroom variables in improving mathematics achievement. *Asian Pacific Education Review, 6*(1), 87–97.

Sezer, R. (2008). Integration of critical thinking skills into elementary school teacher education courses in mathematics. *Education, 3,* 128, 349–362.

Varol, F., & Farran, D. (2006). Early mathematical growth: How to support young children's mathematical development. *Early Childhood Education Journal, 33*(6), 381–387.

Wong, M., & Evans, D. (2007). Improving basic multiplication fact recall for primary school students. *Mathematics Education Research Journal, 19*(1), 89–106.

7

Applications in Algebra, Geometry, and Measurement

A man is like a fraction whose numerator is what he is and whose denominator is what he thinks of himself. The larger the denominator, the smaller the fraction.

Leo Tolstoy

Computation and number sense are important to preparing young learners for mathematical success. However, there is much more to mathematics. As Gersten, Clarke, Haymond, and Jordan (2011) stated, while early number sense should be built wisely, even the best predictors are not perfect in their prediction of math achievement when concepts become more abstract.

Although algebra, geometry, and measurement are combined in this chapter as applications of number sense, they are each important and deserve emphases in an early childhood curriculum. Additionally, although they are separated by definition for ease of explanation, their understanding and application are interrelated. As such, the discussions within this chapter show the connectedness between algebra, geometry, measurement, and number sense.

Key aspects of the chapter:

1. Mastery of formal algebra depends heavily on effective instruction in the primary grades.

2. Focus on rational numbers early.

3. Relate "algebraic" topics to arithmetic properties.

4. Make algebra come alive through measurement and geometry.

Algebra

In a 2007 survey of 743 algebra teachers (Hoffer, Venkataraman, Hedberg, & Shagle, 2007) across the United States, some not-so-surprising results were found. Algebra teachers generally rated their students as ill prepared for algebra understandings with the poorest understandings in rational numbers, word problems, and study habits. Most of the respondents called for a greater focus in primary education on mastery of basic mathematical concepts and skills.

When asked to respond to the question of the most challenging aspect of teaching algebra, 58% of the middle school teachers and 65% of the high school teachers answered "working with unmotivated students." The next most frequent response was "making mathematics accessible and comprehensible to all my students," which was selected by 14% of the middle school and 9% of the high school teachers. When asked to identify the most problematic areas of mathematics that would help prepare students for algebra, teachers responded with several suggestions. The top six areas of preparation problems were (6) integers, (5) solving linear equations, (4) manipulation of variables, (3) rational numbers involving fractions and decimals, (2) basic study habits, and (1) solving word problems. Thus, it is critical that students reach proficiency in the essential areas before they enroll in formal algebra (Gersten, Clarke, & Witzel, 2008).

In a theoretical framework depicting what has been referred to as the arithmetic-to-algebra gap, Witzel, Smith, and Brownell (2001) described the appearance of a barrier to algebraic learning. They found that students with a poor background in mathematics understanding and proficiency would likely have difficulty in algebra. However, even those who appear to succeed in elementary- and middle-level mathematics but still have gaps within their learning risk difficulties with algebra. Prior to a formal algebra course, students must gain facility with computation of whole and rational numbers, along with an understanding of geometric figures, basic graphing, symbols, vocabulary, properties, and procedures. The authors concluded that a strong background in elementary mathematics was necessary but sufficient for success in algebra.

In a systematic review of students' performance when entering algebra, Sanders, Riccomini, and Witzel (2005) used the Algebra Readiness Test to determine areas of relative strength and weakness. In a comparative analysis of students entering a traditional middle-level algebra class with a ninth-grade alternative for those who have performed lower in math, they found both groups were ill prepared in several areas. For both groups, fewer students showed readiness in the three areas of fractions, measurement of geometric figures and objects, and graphical representations. Students in the alternative algebra group evidenced relatively increased difficulty with decimals and exponents, square roots, and scientific notation.

Thus, the best way to improve algebra performance is to build better and more focused instruction before formalized algebra instruction. The first area of focus is computational skills. Parkhurst and colleagues (2010) found that "students who can complete basic math computation problems with rapidity are likely to expend less time and effort on math activities and have less math anxiety" (p. 111). Thus, a focus on proficiency, determined by automaticity of basic facts, particularly in multiplication and multiplicative properties, will have an impact on algebra performance. Moreover, "those with greater basic-fact fluency are more likely to choose to engage in math activities, which further enhance skills" (Parkhurst et al., 2010, p. 111). Woodward (2006) also pushed the need for automaticity of basic facts, stating, "without the ability to retrieve facts directly or automatically, students are likely to experience a high cognitive load as they perform a range of complex tasks" (p. 269).

Another area of focus should be on rational numbers. In its preliminary report, the National Mathematics Advisory Panel (2008) concluded, "By the nature of algebra, the most important among them is proficiency with fractions (including decimals, percent, and negative fractions). The teaching of fractions must be acknowledged as critically important and improved before an increase in student achievement in algebra can be expected" (p. 19). Thus, it is important that students understand and can operationally compute fractions and decimals, ratios, and percents before formalized algebra instruction.

Bright Beginnings

With overwhelming evidence that algebra success is dependent on earlier understanding, it is important to build student thinking to improve the opportunity for achievement. The National Council of Teachers of Mathematics (NCTM) has encouraged algebra instruction as early as possible, going as far as to implement algebra standards for kindergartners. With good intentions, teachers used alternative symbols and wording to justify the introduction of algebra. For symbolic teaching, Kieran (1992) believed the best method to teach the concept of algebraic notation is to teach math symbols as a separate language. Instruction on the definition and utility of symbols, such as = means "is the same as" and × should be · or)(means "groups of," helps build understandings within algebraic equations. In a similar vein, when introducing equations and expressions, such as $3x + 4y$, Kinzel (1999) urged teachers to explicitly teach how to identify and label variables in an expression in preparation for and transition to algebraic manipulations. NCTM's *Principles and Standards* (1989) addressed this issue by stressing the proactive use of letters within equations in Grades 5 through 8 to prepare students for the concept of variables representing numbers in equations.

Connections to the Common Core

In the Common Core State Standards (CCSS), progressions are designed to focus on computational fluency with connections to relationships between operations as well as applications of properties. For example, in kindergarten, students are to learn general definitions and actions of addition and subtraction and then gain fluency to sums of 5. In first grade, students learn the commutative property of addition (if $4 + 6 = 10$, then $6 + 4 = 10$) and the associative property of addition ($6 + 4 + 3 = 6 + 7 = 13$). Also in first grade, students learn that subtraction is not just a take-away operation but can be used an unknown-added problem ($7 + \square = 12$ is the same as $12 - 7 = \square$). By third grade, students are using the associative, commutative, and distributive with multiplication and division and learning that division is not just a measurement or partitive problem but also has an unknown factor ($42 \div \square = 6$ is the same as $6 \bullet \square = 42$). The former discussion that algebra is about patterns and they are to be learned in kindergarten through alternating colored tiles is not emphasized as much. In fact, patterns are not introduced until third grade within the CCSS and thus are more calculation intensive. That said, numeric patterns should be taught early and may be built through the use of the number line and 100s grid so that students can see addition and subtraction patterns.

Solving Algebra Equations

Algebra is not much more than a complex look at arithmetic. Thus, if we use computational concepts to teach algebra and algebraic equations, then students are likely to see the connections more clearly. For example, if I ask a third-grade student to simplify the expression $3x + 4y - 2x$, it is unlikely that she will understand the format of the question let alone come to a reasonable conclusion. However, if I ask a student to simplify what I have—3 red cars, 4 trucks, take away 2 red cars—then she will have a likelihood of answering the question with some reasoning. The difficulty with algebra has much to do with the vocabulary used as well as the computation involved. As described in Chapter 5, if a student has an understanding of place value, that knowledge can be used to help guide work with algebraic expressions as well. For example, what is three 100s plus four 10s minus two 100s? When one of my children was in the beginning of first grade, she used to play math number games with her teacher, asking such questions as "What is four thousand plus two thousand plus fifty?" Acting puzzled, her teacher would provide an answer incorrectly, allowing her to yell out, "Six thousand fifty!" It is this place value understanding that has helped her with word problems, computation, and, yes, algebra.

Missing Addend

Working from the understanding of fact families, students can transition to algebraic equations simply by adapting the number sentence to show the real definition of "equals": "is the same as." Set up a system to help show what happens algebraically. Start by using a frame to represent "what" to show the appearance of an algebra equation with a missing addend. Next, introduce a variable as a letter and set what the letter is equal to. Even, and maybe especially, for those students who quickly know the answer is 4, it is important to see the reasoning.

Question:	5 plus what is 9?
Number sentence:	$5 + \underline{\quad} = 9$
Algebraic manipulation:	$-5 \qquad -5$
	$\underline{\quad} = 9 - 5$
	$\underline{\quad} = 4$
Check:	$5 + \underline{4} = 9$

Question:	12 is what plus 5?
Number sentence:	$12 = \underline{\quad} + 5$
Algebraic manipulation:	$-5 \qquad -5$
	$12 - 5 = \underline{\quad}$
	$7 = \underline{\quad}$
Check:	$12 = \underline{7} + 5$

Missing Subtrahend and Minuend

Similar to solving for a missing addend, set up a system for solving for the unknown. Use a frame instead of a variable until students are more proficient in their procedures.

Missing Minuend

Question:	What minus 4 is 7?
Number sentence:	$\underline{\quad} - 4 = 7$
Algebraic manipulation:	$+ 4 + 4$
	$\underline{\quad} = 7 + 4$
	$\underline{\quad} = 11$
Check:	$\underline{11} - 4 = 7$

Missing Subtrahend

Question:	9 minus what number is 3?
Number sentence:	$9 - \underline{\quad} = 3$
Algebraic manipulation:	$-9 \qquad -9$
	$-\underline{\quad} = 3 - 9$
	$-\underline{\quad} = -6$
	$-1\,(-\underline{\quad}) = -1\,(-6)$
	$+\underline{\quad} = +6$
Check:	$9 - 6 = 3$

Keep the same pattern as completed with missing addends but be advised that students must understand negatives first.

If the students are less familiar with negative numbers, then choose another way to initially introduce solving for missing subtrahends. However, be advised that this alters the pattern from missing addends.

Building Through Geometry and Measurement

Algebra may seem quite difficult for students to understand, particularly at early ages. However, teachers can introduce the algebraic manipulations through physical and pictorial means. Using geometry and measurement concepts, many of the algebraic concepts and manipulations can be initiated. Standards, such as *CCSS 2.MD.4. Measure to determine how much longer one object is than another,* allow students to physically set up equations that can be completed algebraically. To teach missing minuends, a student can use a ruler in place of a number line to show the difference "9 minus what number is 3?" To integrate *CCSS 2.MD.1. Measure the length of an object by selecting and using appropriate tools such as rulers, yardsticks, meter sticks, and measuring tapes,* students could be presented with two different-length objects and asked to identify the difference. This physical work could progress to a possible algebraic equation, such as a missing addend, to show the comparison "L_1 + difference = L_2," where L_1 is a shorter length and L_2 is a longer length.

Using a thermometer, students could solve "35 degrees is how much warmer than 20 degrees?" By creating a construction paper thermometer, students can use red yarn to show the difference. Their movement from one temperature to the next would show a difference of 15 degrees. The teacher could then initiate a conversation about algebra by matching their work to the equation $35 - x = 20$.

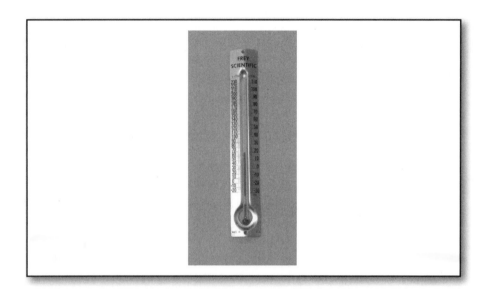

Direct Connections to Computation

Even without the algebraic progression, it is clear to see how measurement and geometry can be used to support the learning of number and computation. Rulers, scales, thermometers, and decibel meters are all tools used in measurement. Each of these can be tracked on a number line, directly tying measurement to numbers and operations. Thus, as students develop number sense, they can learn using units of measurement in activities and math labs that require the application of operations and computation. Certainly, many people have used cooking to introduce fractions connected to measurement. Such measurement standards—*2.MD.5. Use addition and subtraction within 100 to solve word problems involving lengths that are given in the same units, e.g., by using drawings (such as drawings of rulers) and equations with a symbol for the unknown number to represent the problem, and 2.MD.6. Represent whole numbers as lengths from 0 on a number line diagram with equally spaced points corresponding to the numbers 0, 1, 2, . . . , and represent whole-number sums and differences within 100 on a number line diagram*—are designed specifically to connect rulers and measurement instruments to a number line for showing addition and subtraction.

Moreover, geometry standards, such as *3.MD.5. Recognize area as an attribute of plane figures and understand concepts of area measurement,* and *3.MD.7. Relate area to the operations of multiplication and addition,* are designed to show connections of geometric properties and diagrams to multiplication and division.

The geometric progression to fractions is quite clear. In the second grade, students are required to *2.G.2. Partition a rectangle into rows and columns of same-size squares and count to find the total number of them.* This requires learning the definition of division: Equal parts of an object or sum can be partitively grouped or measured to determine the number of equal parts. Using partitive division (Hatfield, Edwards, Bitter, & Morrow, 2008), students split a rectangle into equal pieces.

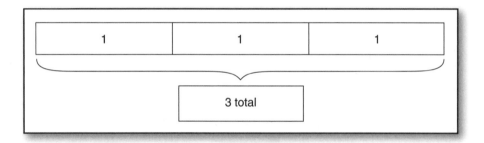

To further students' knowledge, ask them to divide the rectangle into six equal parts. Then, have them name the number of groups of two parts: 6 ÷ 2 = 3 groups of 2. What is unique about physical objects is that 3 does not "magically" show up in the answer, like it would on a calculator. Using a physical manipulation, all three parts of the number sentence are represented: six parts grouped by twos with three groups.

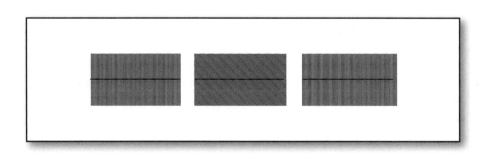

The progression from second to third grade within the CCSS allows a similar use of arrays and rectangles to introduce fractions. The standard *3.G.2. Partition shapes into parts with equal areas. Express the area of each part as a unit fraction of the whole* is designed to progress from the division use of a rectangle to a fraction interpretation. Like partitive division, this rectangle is split into three sections, but the result is interpreted as three sections of one third each that total the original rectangle. So, rather than $3 \div 3 = 1$ per section, students learn $1 \div 3 = \frac{1}{3}$. In both problems, each part of the whole is equally sized.

Hands-on Work Connected Within the Standards

Math should be exciting and often is for students who succeed. For students who are not yet proficient, motivation is important. In the National Survey of Algebra Teachers (Hoffer et al., 2007), algebra teachers reported that motivation was one of the biggest obstacles they faced. By the time students reach secondary mathematics, they have already lost much of their desire to learn. This may be due to lack of relevance or lack of skills to keep up with content. Either way, math needs to be interactive. When teachers employ educational hands-on activities, not only do students increase their engagement and interaction with mathematics, but they also improve their attitudes toward mathematics. At least in the early grades, the CCSS include hands-on activities, particularly within the geometry and measurement standards. The following is a sample of standards and activities that support the need for high amounts of student-student and student-math interaction.

In the CCSS, kindergartners compare two objects using measurable attributes such as weight and length. For example, a recreational ball and an equally sized medicine ball could be used in class to describe how two objects differ in one attribute and not another. This same approach can be made with standard *K.MD.2. Directly compare two objects with a measurable attribute in common, to see which object has "more of"/"less of" the attribute, and describe the difference.* Students can directly compare the lengths of two objects by placing them side by side or even the heights of two people by having them stand back to back. This comparison could be used to build understanding of number magnitude comparisons, an important aspect of early numeracy and a frequent component of number sense assessments (Gersten et al., 2011).

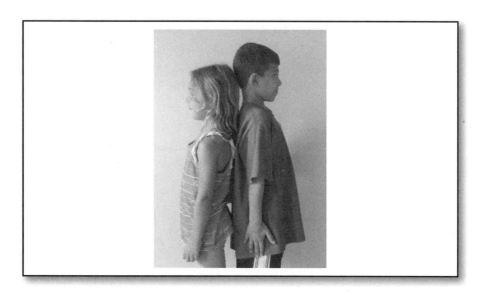

Also in the CCSS, students are to *K.G.5. Model shapes in the world by building shapes from components (e.g., sticks and clay balls) and drawing shapes.* Creating 3D models to show representations of solids could be followed by using nets to help students relate 2D drawings with 3D solids. This is a complex connection for many students, so repeated use and even possibly manipulating foldables that allow a student to physically work between 2D nets and 3D objects will likely be needed.

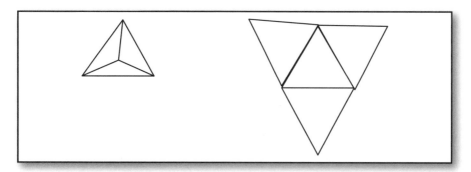

Continued work with shapes and attributes continue into first grade by having students *1.G.1 Build and draw shapes to possess defining attributes* and then into third grade by helping students *(3.G.1) learn that shapes in different categories (e.g., rhombuses, rectangles) may share attributes (e.g., number of sides), and those attributes define a larger category (e.g., quadrilaterals). From this knowledge, students should learn to recognize examples of quadrilaterals, and draw examples of quadrilaterals that do not belong to any of these subcategories.*

Students should learn to distinguish quadrilaterals from other shapes. In the example below, a student drew shapes to create an activity for other students called "Which Does Not Belong?" Peers might exchange similar activities to challenge peers on examples of quadrilaterals.

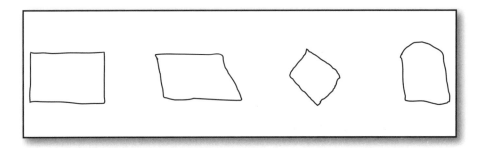

New apps are arriving to help students learn and practice geometric shapes and measurement (see Table 7.1). Although the activities within the apps are becoming much more interactive and easier for younger students to follow, these tools are more effective after children learn from instruction with concrete examples. Think of these apps as opportunities for practice.

Table 7.1   Sample Geometry and Measurement Apps for Use in an iPod or iPad

Sample Geometry Apps for Use in an iPod or iPad		
Application	*Usefulness*	*Cautions*
Geometry 4 Kids by Nth Fusion, LLC, in 2011 ($0.99)	Applications were designed for ages 5 through 10 in the areas of • 2D and 3D, • faces and sides, • corners, • transformations, • angles and rays, and • symmetry.	Limited presentations of each geometry area, and students can't manipulate objects easily.
01 Kids Builder HD Free by Joy Preschool in 2011 (free)	Interactive screens for ages 3 through 7 where students identify shapes.	The focus is on finding shapes more than learning their attributes.

Sample Measurement App for Use in an iPod or iPad		
Application	*Usefulness*	*Cautions*
Measurement by Emantras, Inc., in 2010 ($0.99)	Cute diagrams provide opportunities to conduct simple comparisons of volume, length, and weight.	Limited to third-party measurements.

Conclusion

Building to algebraic understanding requires thoughtful planning. Computation understanding and practice alone will not fully prepare students in mathematics. Incorporate measurement and geometric work throughout the curriculum to increase student interaction with content and make connections to the physical world. Make many examples and activities regarding geometric properties as well as graphical and measurement depictions of mathematics to help students make sense of mathematical equations.

References

Common Core State Standards for Mathematics. (n.d.). Retrieved June 1, 2011, from the Council of Chief State School Officers and National Governors Association website: http://corestandards.org/assets/CCSSI_Math%20 Standards.pdf

Gersten, R., Clarke, B., Haymond, K., & Jordan, N. (2011). *Screening for mathematics difficulties in K–3 students.* Portsmouth, NH: RMC Research Corporation, Center on Instruction.

Gersten, R., Clarke, B., & Witzel, B. (2008). Onwards to algebra: The case for mathematics interventions for struggling students in the intermediate grades. *Compass Learning.* Retrieved June 6, 2012, http://www .compasslearning.com/docs/62MathEmail.pdf

Hatfield, M. M., Edwards, N. T., Bitter, G. G., & Morrow, J. (2008). *Mathematics methods for elementary and middle school teachers* (7th ed.). New York: Wiley.

Hoffer, T. B., Venkataraman, L., Hedberg, E. C., & Shagle, S. (2007). *Final report on the National Survey of Algebra Teachers for the National Math Panel.* Chicago: National Opinion Research Center at the University of Chicago. Retrieved June 6, 2012, http://www2.ed.gov/about/bdscomm/list/ mathpanel/final-report-algebra-teachers.pdf

Kieran, C. (1992). The learning and teaching of school algebra. In D. A. Grouws (Ed.), *Handbook of research on mathematics teaching and learning* (pp. 390–419). New York: Macmillan.

Kinzel, M. T. (1999). Understanding algebraic notation from the students' perspective. *The Mathematics Teacher, 92*(5), 436–442.

National Council of Teachers of Mathematics. (1989). *Principles and standards for school mathematics.* Available from http://www.nctm.org/standards/content.aspx?id=26798

National Mathematics Advisory Panel. (2008). *Foundations for success: The final report of the National Mathematics Advisory Panel.* Washington, DC: U.S. Department of Education. Retrieved June 6, 2012, from http://www2.ed.gov/about/bdscomm/list/mathpanel/report/final-report.pdf

Parkhurst, J., Skinner, C. H., Yaw, J., Poncy, B., Adcock, W., & Luna, E. (2010). Efficient class-wide remediation: Using technology to identify idiosyncratic math facts for additional automaticity drill. *International Journal of Behavioral Consultation and Therapy, 6*(2), 111–123.

Sanders, S., Riccomini, P. R., & Witzel, B. S. (2005). The algebra readiness of high school students in South Carolina: Implications for middle school math teachers. *South Carolina Middle School Journal, 13,* 45–47.

Witzel, B. S., Smith, S. W., & Brownell, M. T. (2001). How can I help students with learning disabilities in algebra? *Intervention in School and Clinic, 37,* 101–104.

Woodward, J. (2006). Developing automaticity in multiplication facts: Integrating strategy instruction with timed practice drills. *Learning Disabilities Quarterly, 29,* 269–289.

8

Using Math Language to Solve Problems

If the world is becoming flat, then children should become fluent with several means of communication. One of those had better be math.

Bradley S. Witzel

Proficiency in numbers and operations allows people the ability to work with and excel in real-life applications. For example, when a student understands computation, then it is possible to apply that understanding to such important skills as computing interest on a loan or predicting inventory needs. In many households, for example, such applications are emphasized. From grocery store trips to nature walks and museum visits, the applications of mathematics can be made obvious. However, in some households, there are few attempts at connecting mathematics to everyday life, and in many cases, math applications are not as readily apparent to students as most teachers would hope. Even in households where math is emphasized, families may have difficulty showing how and why math is used on a daily basis. Thus, school mathematics may be the only time during the day for many students when math has meaning.

To make math meaningful, it is important to teach math as a language and to explicitly emphasize math applications. Role playing, vignettes, and interactive structured play are some of the many ways to use mathematics. With the increased emphasis on math applications, many textbooks have responded by increasing the number of problems solving events and questions. Most of the textbook additions come in the form of word problems. In addition to the increased emphasis on word problems are activities and lab-type questions throughout textbooks. In many cases, what once were considered *extras* to a math unit are now considered *essentials* that should not be bypassed.

> "Teachers are encouraged to use a variety of problems intentionally and to ensure that students have the language and mathematical content knowledge necessary to solve the problems" (Woodward et al., 2012, p. 10).

While it may seem obvious that teachers must use word problems and applications, what is less obvious is that students need to learn how to read and work within the language of mathematics. Too often, students who appear to struggle in mathematics experience difficulties in reading (Jordan, Hanich, & Kaplan, 2003). Students' performance in mathematics is directly affected by their performance in reading as reading is a predictor of mathematics failure in the classroom (Fletcher, 2005). In a review of the National Assessment of Educational Progress, the National Mathematics Advisory Panel (2008) found that interpreting students' math scores includes "many flaws" and "nonmathematical sources of influence" (p. 60). One possible reason for possible misinterpretation is the heavy use of reading and language in mathematics assessments. Students must learn mathematics vocabulary in order to understand class instruction, read word problems, and eventually solve problems on statewide exams.

Math textbooks have a history of questionable readability (Prins & Ulijn, 1998; Witzel, 2009). While many publishers report the Lexile readability to show the appropriateness per grade level, what really matters is the range of readability across a textbook. In other words, if a textbook is written at the second-grade level, it may range in readability from the kindergarten- through fifth-grade level. Thus, although a textbook adoption committee may determine a textbook as appropriate for a certain grade level or even for a specific group of learners, the student may only be able to read a portion of the textbook. This affects how much of the directions that the student, or even parents, can read and how many of the word problems the student truly understands.

To determine the readability range of textbooks, an urban school district textbook adoption committee conducted a readability analysis on two third- and fifth-grade textbooks using a Fry scale. The strength of the Fry scale is that it provides an overall impression and can cover lower grades (Fry, 2002). However, a Fry scale only gives whole-grade reading levels, rather than sublevels, which may inflate the grade level when passages use multisyllabic mathematics words repeatedly (Shorrocks-Taylor & Hargreaves, 2000). Still, the Fry scale is an often-used instrument in textbook evaluation (Lowry & Moser, 1995).

Using a technique conducted by Witzel (2009) in his work with middle-level and algebra textbooks, the committee randomly selected different standards in the third- and fifth-grade curriculum. Then the lead consultant completed a Fry scale interpretation on both directions and word problems of those appropriately aligned sections of textbooks from two different publishers. Similar to the results of Witzel, the result of this analysis revealed a wide range of readability scores both between textbooks and within textbooks. The wide range of readability of each textbook suggests that the directions of the textbooks are written not for students at the indicated grade, but rather for definitional correctness. For the purpose of showing the reading-level range per textbook, the publishers' names are omitted in Table 8.1.

Table 8.1 Textbook Range of Readability

Grade	Textbook Publisher	Area of Textbook Sampled	Directions Readability Range	Word Problems Readability Range
3	Publisher A	2-digit addition, perpendicular lines, lines, angles, and fractions	2nd–5th	4th–6th
3	Publisher B		6th–8th	2nd–6th
5	Publisher A	Determining the solution and least common multiple	8th–9th	4th–6th
5	Publisher B		6th–7th	3rd–6th

As shown in Table 8.1, the sampled readabilities are often widely varied and misaligned with their respective student grade level. The third-grade scores are more widely varied, likely because we sampled a larger number of standards. The fifth-grade scores are simply too high for the expected reading level of the students. There are several ways to interpret these scores about the inappropriateness of directions and word problems with current textbooks. However, it is quite difficult to keep a steady reading level for every math standard, especially considering the complex math vocabulary that students must learn.

We encourage textbook adoption committees to assess the reading level of potential textbooks and to best align their selection with the reading level of their students. Even with the most appropriate textbook, schools and districts have little to no say in the readability of directions and word problems included in statewide assessments. Thus, it is important to teach students strategies and approaches that will help them better understand the language of mathematics.

Math Language

Math is considered by many to be a separate language. Even with vocabulary as seemingly simple as numbers, there are obvious roadblocks. To a student, 45 sounds like "four-T five." A student might interpret this as "four T," for four 10s, and five 1s. This is similar for numbers in the 60s, 70s, 80s, and 90s. However, for numbers in the 20s, 30s, and 50s, the student may be left searching for the numeral that represents the "twens," "thirs," and "fifs."

Throughout this book, from the place value chapter (Chapter 5) to the integrated lesson samples, the math language we use may appear different from what appears in current math textbooks and certainly different from how many of us learned mathematics language. Within the Common Core State Standards (CCSS) for math, there is usually a consistent use of math language. For example, number identification uses place value language as number of 10s and number of 1s (e.g., 43 is four 10s plus three 1s). However, in other areas, the language fluctuates per vocabulary term. In those cases, the point is to show the terms as synonyms. We recommend studying the progressions in this book to see how to develop the math and accurate language of mathematics. One example is with progressing from counting to multiplication. In kindergarten, the standard reads to count by 1s. Then, in first grade, the standard reads to work with counting and multiples. The standard in second grade reads to skip count and then by third grade is back to multiples. While it would make more sense to use the language of multiples rather than skip counting, the point is to help students learn that counting by multiple numbers is to work with multiples. Knowing this, first- and second grade-teachers should use the word *multiples* when teaching what was previously called skip counting.

CCSS counting language mixed sequence:

K.CC.1. Count to 100 by ones and by tens.

K.CC.2. Count forward beginning from a given number within the known sequence (instead of having to begin at 1).

1.OA.5. Relate counting to addition and subtraction (e.g., by counting on 2 to add 2).

1.NBT.4. Add within 100, including adding a two-digit number and a one-digit number, and adding a two-digit number and a multiple of 10, using concrete models or drawings and strategies based on place value, properties of operations, and/or the relationship between addition and subtraction; relate the strategy to a written method and explain the reasoning used. Understand that in adding two-digit numbers, one adds tens and tens, ones and ones; and sometimes it is necessary to compose a ten.

2.NBT.2. Count within 1,000; skip-count by 5s, 10s, and 100s.

3.NBT.3. Multiply one-digit whole numbers by multiples of 10 in the range 10–90 (e.g., 9 × 80, 5 × 60) using strategies based on place value and properties of operations.

To help students make the transition to this increased use of math language, it is important to explicitly teach math vocabulary. From an intensive review of research, the Institute of Education Sciences math problem–solving panel concluded that "academic language, including the language used in mathematics, should be taught explicitly so that all students understand what is being asked in a problem and how the problem should be solved" (Woodward et al., 2012, p. 16). Students can keep a journal of math language recording the term and definition that they can refer to later. However, such a journal would not be as beneficial as the terms are simply copied from the book to the journal. The journal should contain interpretations and paraphrased definitions that explain the mathematics vocabulary in a manner that more appropriately suits the need of each learner.

Triple-Entry Journal

Use a triple-entry journal to organize student learning of vocabulary. The use of a triple-entry journal particularly helps students who have not yet learned a strategy to take notes on math vocabulary that aids their memory. Triple-entry journals start with the teacher introducing a math term and explaining the relevance of the term to mathematics and to students socially. The students then write the term, write their own definition of the term, and finally draw a picture or diagram to help them remember it. The teacher then reviews students' work and provides feedback to clarify any misconceptions and support the accurate descriptions. In the modified triple-entry journal example below, the teacher introduces the term *addend* and shows where addends are in a math sentence and how they are used for problem solving (CCSS—2.OA.3. Determine whether a group of objects [up to 20] has an odd or even number of members, e.g., by pairing objects or counting them by 2s; write an equation to express an even number as a sum of two equal addends). Students then fill out their triple-entry journal on the term and have the teacher review it.

Word	In My Own Words	Number Explanation
Addend	A number that is added in an addition problem. An addend plus an addend is a sum.	**8 addend** **+ 8 addend** 16

In Chapter 9, we discuss specific explicit instructional strategies for teaching mathematics vocabulary.

Word Problems

Understanding vocabulary is necessary but not sufficient for solving word problems. Students must be able to determine what word problems are asking and how to approach it. This requires reading comprehension and analysis as well as the requisite math skills to perform accurately. There are several similarities to teaching reading comprehension and math word problems. Similarities required in teaching approaches may include the following:

- organization within the strategy used,
- understanding before answering questions,
- multiple formats of interaction,

- identification of extraneous and unrelated information, and
- a need for the passage to come alive.

In order to teach students to solve word problems, students need an organizational approach. Even those who seem to solve it in their heads really have an approach to decode, comprehend, design a strategy, and solve the problem. Reading the word problem is not enough. Decoding is a good start, but students should be able to retell or paraphrase the word problem. Using multiple formats of interactions means to give students the opportunity to ask and answer questions about the problem. This can be done by discussing the problem with other students or the teacher. Another way to develop an interaction is to draw pictures or diagrams that make better sense of the problem and even make it come alive. When you make sense of the problem, you should be able to identify what doesn't belong, thus eliminating the extraneous information in the problem. Finally, if the problem involves a context unfamiliar to the students, then it is likely that the students will understand how to identify what is important and what is extraneous in the problem. Even when teaching mathematics, you are also teaching reading.

Math in Context

Using scenarios and situations where mathematics is present helps students see the relationship of mathematics to real-world contexts. Additionally, if number sentences are set up in a manner that matches the word sentence, then the translation may show better connections to conversational language more familiar to students. In the examples below are three math sentences that translate from and into word sentences. In the first example, the object or unit stays consistent. This is typically true of addition and subtraction. For multiplication and division, however, it is slightly different. With multiplication, it is the total number of units or objects that forms the product. In division, the form of the problem may show the partitive answer. In this example, the question is cars per lot, and the answer is cars per lot.

8 bears	5 bunches of 4 bananas each = 20 bananas	12 cars ÷ 6 lots = 2 cars per lot
− 3 bears		or $2 \, ^{cars}/_{lot}$
5 bears		

Stepwise Strategies

With reading research becoming more apparent across the curriculum, fewer teachers than ever are asking students to answer questions without any strategy. Most general word problem strategies include such steps as these:

1. Read for understanding.

2. Develop a strategy to solve the problem.

3. Show steps to solve the problem.

4. Check the reasonableness of the answer.

While these are good steps, they only begin to explain the usefulness and possibilities of word problem strategies. One of the most generic approaches is the reading comprehension strategy translated to mathematics, KWS. The steps to KWS are (1) what do we *know* about the problem, (2) what do we *want* to know, and (3) what *strategy* do we use to solve the problem? These simple steps have been adapted in multiple ways, such as Problem, Strategy, Solve, and Check, to organize students' approaches to solving word problems.

Other more involved strategies include such ideas as the following:

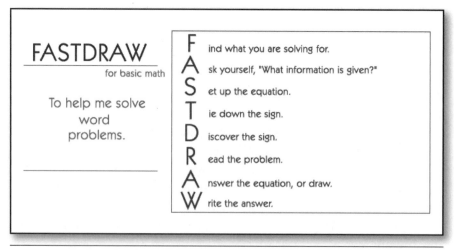

Source: http://coe.jmu.edu/learningtoolbox

Websites like the Learning Toolbox even show how to complete the strategy step by step explicitly. The Learning Toolbox even has links for parents and students to learn how to implement the strategy.

Montague (2003) used the Solve It! method to help students solve word problems in several successful studies. Essentially, the steps to solve it include the following:

- Read (for understanding)
- Paraphrase (your own words)
- Visualize (a picture or a diagram)
- Hypothesize (a plan to solve the problem)
- Estimate (predict the answer)
- Compute (do the arithmetic)
- Check (make sure everything is right)

What is unique about Montague's approach is the use of a picture to make sense of the problem before solving it. Jitendra and her colleagues (2007) found that students who used diagrams and pictorial connections to strategies had higher scores on word problem solving when compared to more general strategies above. Montague, Enders, and Dietz (2011) found that teaching strategies to solve word problems benefit not only young learners but adolescents as well. All students must have a strategic approach that organizes their approach to word problems and shows them how best to solve the problem.

Figure 8.1

Schema-Based

For students who struggle the most, it is important that they learn specific strategies that teach the structure of word problems. In other words, students need to learn to identify semantic cues in problems and be able to draw the relationship described in the problem (Jitendra, George, Sood, & Price, 2010). A semantic cue in a word problem would be the recognition of a noun or verb that can be translated from a word sentence to a number sentence. In the word problem below from Gersten and his colleagues (2009), both Brad and Madhavi must be recognized as people having bottle caps in order for the student to recognize that there is a difference between how much each person has. These authors concluded, "Interventions should include instruction on solving word problems that is based on common underlying structures" (Gersten et al., 2009, p. 26). Teaching underlying structures means to teach schema-based problem-solving strategies.

The two problems below are addition and subtraction problems that students may be tempted to solve using an incorrect operation. In each case, students can draw a simple diagram like the one shown below, record the known quantities (two out of three of A, B, and C), and then use the diagram to decide whether addition or subtraction is the correct operation to use to determine the unknown quantity.

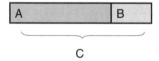

1. Brad has a bottle cap collection. After Madhavi gave Brad 28 more bottle caps, Brad had 111 bottle caps. How many bottle caps did Brad have before Madhavi gave him more?
2. Brad has a bottle cap collection. After Brad gave 28 of his bottle caps to Madhavi, he had 83 bottle caps left. How many bottle caps did Brad have before he gave Madhavi some?

Source: Gersten et al. (2009).

For early grades, there are three general types of problem-solving schema: change, compare, and group. As students progress, they learn more strategies that show multiplicative properties and proportional reasoning. For the purpose of this book, we focus on the underlying structures used in early grades. In a change problem, a quantity is presented followed by an action verb that either increases or decreases the quantity to lead to an unknown amount. A compare problem involves the presentation of two quantities of similar type where one number is larger than the other and a difference is being sought. In a group problem, two quantities of different type are presented. Then, these two smaller quantities are grouped together to make a larger one.

Students are taught to identify what type of problem they are reading. Next, students are taught to pictorially represent the problem. The pictorial representation is more commonly a strip diagram that resembles a number line. Once the pictorial representation of the problem is developed, the student solves the problem and then checks the reasonableness of the answer. See below for examples of each of the three early grades' underlying structures.

a. A change problem could be "For Mother's Day, Laura placed 18 flowers in a vase. Caroline put in 13 more. How many flowers are in the vase?"

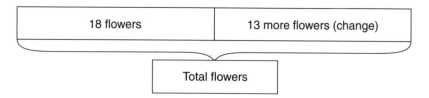

b. A compare problem may read as "Tyler received 12 presents. Andrea received 7. How many more presents did Tyler receive?"

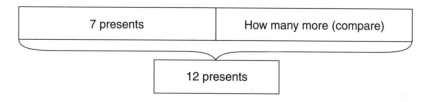

c. A group problem may read as "Jose has 3 cats at his home. Manuel's family has 4 dogs. How many pets do they have altogether?"

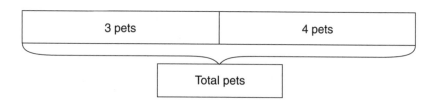

Teaching students a means for solving word problems alleviates some of the frustration and resistance that students exhibit when challenged with reading and mathematics. The consistency of the stepwise and visual approach aids students who have not established a way to solve problems. As we have emphasized throughout this book, one area of math connects to another. For example, consider CCSS—2.MD.4. Measure to determine how much longer one object is than another, expressing the length difference in terms of a standard length unit. This standard ties directly to the use of strip diagrams within schema-based problem solving.

Word Problem Apps

Reading about mathematics in context, such as the newspaper or magazines or select books, is a good way of understanding mathematics applications. However, reading about mathematics does not necessarily prepare students for mathematics problem solving in a word problem format. Use of apps can help students practice word problem–solving approaches. There are a limited number of apps devoted to word problem solving (see Table 8.2). Continue reviewing new apps for word problem solving to provide more opportunities for students to succeed.

As students progress and problems become more complex, so must the approaches to helping students with mathematics

Table 8.2 Sample Word Problem App for Use in an iPod or iPad

Application	Usefulness	Cautions
RoboLearning: Math Word Problems 1 by David R. Fox in 2011 ($1.99)	Presents word problems on an illustrated robot, is inviting, and includes problems that are fairly straightforward.	Does not show how to solve problems, includes no visuals other than the robot's picture, and presents answers in a multiple-choice format.

language. We must model accurate and efficient problem solving using think-alouds to help our students build their own proficiency. Researched approaches, like the ones presented in this chapter, will help students. However, with research still in its early stages, more vocabulary and word problem–solving techniques and approaches are needed for elementary to secondary settings. Continue to practice action research and review research journals for the latest developments. The worst thing we can do with math language is to ignore it.

References

Common Core State Standards for Mathematics. (n.d.). Retrieved June 1, 2011, from the Council of Chief State School Officers and the National Governors Association website: http://corestandards.org/assets/CCSSI_Math%20Standards.pdf

Fletcher, J. M. (2005). Predicting math outcomes: Reading predictors and comorbidity. *Journal of Learning Disabilities, 38,* 308–312.

Fry, E. (2002). Readability versus leveling. *Reading Teacher, 56,* 286–291.

Gersten, R., Beckmann, S., Clarke, B., Foegen, A., Marsh, L., Star, J. R., & Witzel, B. (2009). *Assisting students struggling with mathematics: Effective response to intervention (RTI) for elementary and middle schools* (NCEE 2009-4060). Washington, DC: National Center for Education Evaluation and Regional Assistance, Institute of Education Sciences, U.S. Department of Education. Retrieved from http://ies.ed.gov/ncee/wwc/publications/practiceguides

Jitendra, A. K. (2008). *Solving math word problems.* Austin, TX: Pro-Ed.

Jitendra, A. K., George, M. P., Sood, S., & Price, K. (2010). Schema-based instruction: Facilitating mathematical word problem solving for students with emotional and behavioral disorders. *Preventing School Failure, 54*(3), 145–151.

Jitendra, A. K., Griffin, C. C., Haria, P., Leh, J., Adams, A., & Kaduvettoor, A. (2007). A comparison of single and multiple strategy instruction on third-grade students' mathematical problem solving. *Journal of Educational Psychology, 99*(1), 115–127.

Jordan, N. C., Hanich, L. B., & Kaplan, D. (2003). A longitudinal study of mathematical competencies in children with specific mathematics difficulties versus children with comorbid mathematics and reading difficulties. *Child Development, 74,* 834–850.

Lowry, J. R., & Moser, W. C. (1995). Textbook selections: A multi-step approach. *Marketing Education Review, 5*(3), 21–28.

Montague, M. (2003). *Solve It!: A mathematical problem-solving instructional program.* Reston, VA: Exceptional Innovations.

Montague, M., Enders, C., & Dietz, S. (2011). Effects of cognitive strategy instruction on math problem solving of middle school students with learning disabilities. *Learning Disability Quarterly, 34*(4), 262–272.

National Mathematics Advisory Panel. (2008). *Foundations for success: The final report of the National Mathematics Advisory Panel.* Washington, DC: U.S. Department of Education. Retrieved from http://www.ed.gov/MathPanel

Prins, E. D., & Ulijn, J. M. (1998). Linguistic and cultural factors in the *readability* of *mathematics* texts: The Whorfian hypothesis revisited with evidence from the South African context. *Journal of Research in Reading, 21,* 139–159.

Shorrocks-Taylor, D., & Hargreaves, M. (2000). Measuring the language demands of mathematics tests: The case of the statutory tests for 11-year-olds in England and Wales. *Assessment in Education: Principles, Policy, and Practice, 7,* 39–60.

Witzel, B. S. (2009). Beware of homework: Dealing with the interference of textbook readability. *Focus on Middle School, 22*(2), 1–4.

Woodward, J., Beckmann, S., Driscoll, M., Franke, M., Herzig, P., Jitendra, A., Koedinger, K. R., & Ogbuehi, P. (2012). Improving mathematical problem solving in Grades 4 through 8: A practice guide (NCEE 2012-4055). Washington, DC: National Center for Education Evaluation and Regional Assistance, Institute of Education Sciences, U.S. Department of Education. Retrieved from http://ies.ed.gov/ncee/wwc/publications_reviews.aspx#pubsearch/

9

Mathematical Vocabulary and the Development of Early Mathematicians

Language forces us to perceive the world as man presents it to us.

Julia Penelope

Vocabulary understanding is uniformly recognized as a major contributor to students' overall comprehension and general knowledge. The importance of developing a proper and thorough mathematical vocabulary base is an essential aspect of teaching mathematics to young children. Proficiency in mathematics depends on a continuous growth and blend of intricate combinations of critical component skills such as concepts, procedures, algorithms, computation, problem solving, and language (Riccomini, Sanders, & Jones, 2008). If students do not understand the language of instruction, students will struggle to learn during mathematics instruction (Riccomini & Witzel, 2010). Learning and using the language of mathematics, as with language in general, is essential and greatly dependent on vocabulary knowledge.

The language of mathematics uses three linguistic tools—(1) words, (2) symbols, and (3) diagrams—to communicate mathematical concepts, procedures, and relationships. If students are weak or underdeveloped in any of these areas, their overall mathematics learning can be slowed.

Language in mathematics is important because it is necessary for communication, mathematics reasoning, and precision. Students must effortlessly use, understand, and apply mathematical words, symbols, and diagrams routinely during math activities.

In an effort to improve students' overall mathematical performance, educators should recognize the importance of mathematical language and use research-validated instructional methods to teach important mathematical vocabulary. The purpose of this chapter is to provide teachers an overall understanding of the impact of mathematical vocabulary on proficiency and specific evidenced-based instructional strategies to promote the learning of essential vocabulary in mathematics.

In this chapter, we present background research and discuss the implications and importance of vocabulary development during mathematics instruction. We will cover both general instructional recommendations and specific instructional strategies to more effectively teach math vocabulary. Hopefully, after reading this chapter, you will

1. recognize the importance of teaching vocabulary in mathematics.

2. recognize the different challenges and difficulties mathematical vocabulary presents in both teaching and learning.

3. identify and implement both general and specific instruction that can assist in the more effective teaching of mathematical vocabulary.

Vocabulary and Mathematical Proficiency

Although often overlooked, the importance of vocabulary knowledge is receiving a renewed emphasis in the content area of mathematics, especially at the early levels of mathematics instruction. For many years, both the National Council of Teachers of Mathematics (NCTM) and the National Research Council (NRC) have clearly embedded the importance of language development in their definitions of mathematical proficiency.

NCTM (1989, 2000) delineates the importance of language in the five strands necessary for mathematical proficiency, one of which is adaptive reasoning. The adaptive reasoning strand, described as the "capacity for logical thought, reflection, explanation, and justification" (Kilpatrick, Swafford, & Findell, 2001, p. 116) clearly highlights the language component embedded within the idea of proficiency. Similarly, the NRC (Kilpatrick et al., 2001) specifically identified the ability to "engage with mathematics" as the all-around ability to communicate mathematically. More recently, the Common Core State Standards (CCSS) for Mathematics describes 8 standards for mathematical practice that have clearly embedded the importance of vocabulary development to overall mathematical proficiency. Undoubtedly, language development plays an important role in mathematical proficiency. Moreover, if students do not understand the language of instruction, they cannot learn what is being instructed.

Vocabulary acquisition is an important element of instruction in all content-area classrooms (Biemiller, 2004; Marzano, 2004); however, it is often overlooked and underestimated during mathematics instruction. Although students acquire many new words simply through daily math instruction, many students often have a very underdeveloped vocabulary knowledge base and fail to learn even a basic level of vocabulary specific to mathematics. Additionally, students arrive at school with sizable differences in their vocabulary knowledge in general (Hart & Risley, 1995). Further complicating student vocabulary development is the lack of strategic learning skills necessary to acquire new vocabulary during mathematics instruction. Poor vocabulary can become a barrier to students' continued development of conceptual understanding, relationship building, and problem solving required for mathematical proficiency.

Difficulties Students Experience With Mathematical Vocabulary

Researchers have found that many students have limitations in their exposure to vocabulary and language in general. According to Hart and Risley (1995), young children from economically disadvantaged environments hear fewer words than children who come from economically advantaged situations. In an average hour, for example, young children from disadvantaged backgrounds may hear 600 words in a typical hour, while the children from less disadvantaged families heard over 1,200 words and the average child from a professional family heard over 2,100 words. Therefore, the results of the study indicate that children from the highest socioeconomic strata heard almost 4 times as many words in a typical hour than did their least-advantaged peers. The cumulative effect of the limited opportunities to hear spoken language can have a significant negative impact on a child's overall language and vocabulary development. Over the course of two to three years, some students from the most impoverished circumstances will have heard millions of words fewer than their peers from more economically advantaged homes.

Adding to the challenges for students overall language and vocabulary development are the content-heavy areas and the technical vocabulary necessary for students to learn. There are many challenges in learning mathematics. Reading mathematics and communicating mathematically is a complex task that includes comprehension; mathematical understanding and fluency; and proficiency with reading numbers, symbols, words, and diagrams. There are at least eleven specific difficulties students encounter when learning math vocabulary.

It is important to recognize how these difficulties present challenges for students so that we can design instructional strategies and activities to help students overcome these difficulties. According to Rubenstein and Thompson (2002), there are eleven specific difficulties to learning math vocabulary: (1) meanings are context dependent—*right angle* versus *right answer*; (2) mathematical meanings are more precise—*even* as divisible by 2 versus *even* as smooth; (3) terms specific to mathematical contexts—*numerator, hypotenuse, rhombus*; (4) multiple meanings—*square* as the shape versus *square* as a number itself; (5) discipline-specific technical meanings—*variable* as an unknown quantity in an equation versus *variable clouds*; (6) homonyms with everyday words—*arc* versus *ark*; (7) related but different—*hundreds* and *hundredths*; (8) specific challenges with translated words; (9) irregularities in spelling—*four* has a *u*, but *forty* does not; (10) concepts may be verbalized in more than one way—*one-quarter* versus *one-fourth*; and (11) students & teachers adopt informal terms instead of mathematical term—*corner* versus *vertex*.

Table 9.1   Chart of Difficulties for Learning Mathematical Vocabulary

Difficulty	Examples
1. Meanings are context dependent	*Right* angle versus *right* answer
	Right angle versus *right* hand
	Reflection as flipping over a line versus *reflection* as thinking about something
	Foot as 12 inches versus the *foot* on a leg
2. Mathematical meanings are more precise	*Difference* as the answer to a subtraction problem versus *difference* as a general comparison
	Even as divisible by 2 versus *even* as smooth

Difficulty	Examples
3. Terms specific to mathematical contexts	*Quotient, decimal, denominator, quadrilateral, parallelogram, isosceles*
4. Multiple meanings	*Round* as a circle versus *round* a number to the tenths place *Square* as the shape versus *square* as a number itself *Second* as a measure of time versus *second* as a location in a set of ordered pairs A *side* of a rectangle as a line segment versus a *side* of a prism as a rectangle
5. Discipline-specific technical meanings	*Divide* in mathematics means separate into parts, but the *Continental Divide* is a geographical term referring to a ridge that separates eastward- and westward-flowing waters *Variable* in mathematics is a letter that represents possible numerical values, but *variable* clouds in science are a weather condition
6. Homonyms with everyday words	*Sum* versus *some, arc* versus *ark, pi* versus *pie, graphed* versus *graft*
7. Related but different	*Factor* and *multiple, hundreds* and *hundredths, numerator* and *denominator*
8. Challenges with translated words	In Spanish, the table at which we eat is a *mesa*, but a mathematical table is a *tabla*
9. Irregularities in spelling	Four has a *u*, but *forty* does not Fraction denominators, such as *sixth, fifth, fourth,* and *third,* are like ordinal numbers, but rather than *second* the next fraction is *half*
10. Concepts may be verbalized in more than one way	*Skip count by threes* versus *tell the multiples of 3* *One-quarter* versus *one-fourth*
11. Students and teachers adopt informal terms instead of mathematical terms	*Diamond* versus *rhombus* *Corner* versus *vertex* *Bottom number* versus *denominator*

Source: Adapted from Rubenstein & Thompson (2002).

Learning essential mathematical vocabulary is sometimes very difficult with many complex variables impacting learning. Recognizing that vocabulary is an important component in mathematics comprehension and the many difficulties it presents students is only the initial step in the process; effectively teaching vocabulary is the essential next step. It is not enough that students are simply exposed to new vocabulary words; they must completely understand them in order to be successful. Therefore, the purpose of teaching essential vocabulary in mathematics class is threefold. First, the overall goal of vocabulary instruction is to have students store meanings of the words in their long-term memory. Second, once the word meanings are in long-term memory, the goal of vocabulary instruction becomes to help students become proficient and maintain the words' meanings over time. Finally, the end result of achieving Goals 1 and 2 is that students are able to easily and accurately use the language of mathematics to explain and justify mathematical concepts and relationships.

General Approaches and Techniques to Teaching Mathematical Vocabulary

Obviously, vocabulary is being taught during most math classes in some fashion; however, using a systematic and direct approach to teaching vocabulary across the year will maximize and facilitate improved understanding of essential vocabulary with your students. Although this chapter is focusing on mathematical vocabulary, there are important general steps to vocabulary instruction in all content areas. A school can maximize students' learning of essential vocabulary by uniformly following these six general steps to teach vocabulary described by Marzano (2004): (1) provide an informal description, explanation, or example of the new term or phrase; (2) ask students to restate the description, explanation, or example in their own words; (3) ask students to construct a picture, symbol, or graphic representation of the term or phrase; (4) engage students periodically in activities that help them add to their knowledge of the new terms; (5) ask students to periodically discuss terms with one another; and (6) involve students periodically in games that allow them to play with the terms.

If all teachers (science, math, social studies, etc.) are following the same six steps, students are then able to see the connections to learning vocabulary across contexts. These six steps articulated are not necessarily new, but often get pushed to the side during math instruction. Since these six steps are important to all vocabulary instruction, it is important to have these as the foundation. We will now discuss steps essential to teaching mathematical vocabulary.

Although many of the components to teaching vocabulary in other content areas can be applied to mathematics, there are seven critical components for teaching math vocabulary. Adams (2003) describes these important steps: (1) establish a list of vocabulary for each subject area or unit; (2) evaluate comprehension of mathematics vocabulary on a periodic basis; (3) probe students' previous knowledge and usage of important terms before vocabulary is introduced during instruction; (4) frame the context for new mathematics vocabulary; (5) develop an environment where mathematics vocabulary is a normal part of instruction, curriculum, and assessment; (6) encourage students to ask about terms they don't know; and (7) teach students how to find meanings of vocabulary words (e.g., dictionary, Internet, notes). Now that we have laid the foundation for more effective math vocabulary instruction, we will provide a few examples of instructional activities that should be employed more frequently during mathematics class.

Activities for Teaching Math Vocabulary

Keyword Approach

One strategy to learning vocabulary is through the keyword approach (Mastropieri & Scruggs, 2010). Using the keyword approach, students record new and difficult vocabulary terms, write a word or phrase that helps them remember the term and definition, draw a picture of the word association, and then list the meaning of the term. For example, students were learning the definition of the word *plane* (CCSS—K.G.3. Identify shapes as two-dimensional [lying in a plane, "flat"] or three-dimensional ["solid"]) but had difficulty understanding. To show that a plane is a two-dimensional flat surface that extends out forever, students came up with different ways to remember it. One group thought that *plane* sounded similar to the word *plate* and drew a picture of how the plate could be like a plane. Figure 9.1 shows the keyword approach of the term *plane*. By having students create and analyze word associations and definitions of math terms, students are more likely to retain the definition and application of the term.

The Index Card. Another approach to help students remember essential vocabulary words is the use of index cards. This technique is very common in the content area of reading, but often underutilized in mathematics. For example, both of my sons' kindergarten and first-grade teachers would send home index cards of "important reading words" that my sons were to learn. I was always puzzled as to why the index cards never included "important math words." Nonetheless, this technique could easily be applied to math vocabulary words, especially if the student is already using it for reading.

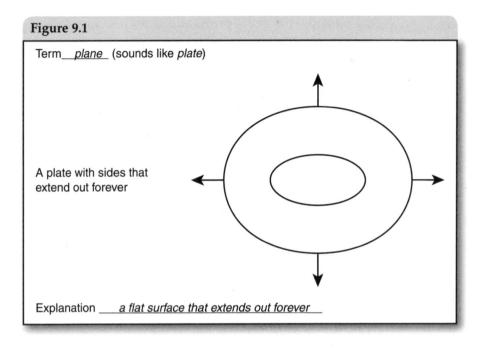

Figure 9.1

Term___*plane*___(sounds like *plate*)

A plate with sides that
extend out forever

Explanation _____*a flat surface that extends out forever*_____

This after-instruction technique tends to work well for students because they have taken the time to write down important information in a convenient and easy-to-study format, on index cards, which they then are able to study any time. For young children, the index cards could consist of illustrations either created by the students or provided by the teacher. The after-instruction practice of vocabulary words is a critical piece of fostering long-term remembering of math vocabulary words.

Unfortunately, many students are not strategic enough to take the initiative on their own to create index cards of essential math vocabulary. The cards will have to made for them. Time may be planned during math class to have students create index cards, or students can create their index cards as part of their homework assignment. Remember, creating the cards is only one minor part of this approach. The most important aspect of the index card approach is the subsequent studying of the cards. Creation alone is not sufficient to promote learning and remembering of the essential vocabulary. The students must use the cards to help themselves remember the information contained on the cards.

Have students study their cards any time, even if it is only for a few seconds; use all available time. They can practice saying the term and defining it as well as using it in different contexts. Set up motivating ways to encourage students to practice math vocabulary, such as requiring students to recite the meaning of a term before they leave the room, sometimes referred to as a "ticket out the door." The index cards can be used to study with a partner, thereby allowing the partners to hold each other accountable for proper use of terms as well as helping clarify difficult or complex terms.

Game Activities. Students should play a variety of vocabulary "games" and fun activities that allow them to promote retention and develop a deeper understanding of the terminology. As previously discussed, one of Marzano's (2004) six steps for effective vocabulary instruction is to provide students periodic opportunities to engage with vocabulary through games. The primary purpose of these games is to engage students in a fun and motivating activity to increase their understanding and retention of essential vocabulary.

Educational games are ideal for engaging students in motivating activities with the purpose of improved understanding of essential vocabulary. Additionally, the majority of students find games to be fun and very helpful. Keep in mind that some students may not enjoy games that involve intense competition and would benefit from just working individually or with a partner to quiz each other about the terms.

Most teachers have established game activities designed to serve various learning objectives. For example, Jeopardy is a very common game format used in many classrooms, not just math classrooms. A benefit of such a game is the potential to use a vocabulary category that continues to grow as students learn more and more terms through the course of the year.

Other game formats that can readily be adjusted to include math vocabulary are as follows:

1. Family Feud—where a student team is asked to list characteristics of vocabulary terms or provide examples and nonexamples.

2. Matching games such as Memory, Concentration, and Bingo—where students are asked to match a term with a definition or characteristics with a term.

3. Trivia games—where students are required to apply their knowledge about certain vocabulary terms.

The main point of including vocabulary in game-like activities is to provide students fun activities to engage in learning and remembering essential vocabulary. If learning math vocabulary is something that is boring or painful, not fun, students will likely avoid it, further reducing their overall math vocabulary knowledge. Teachers can make learning and remembering math vocabulary fun by using a variety of card, board, and other games in math class. The Internet offers a wealth of free and easily accessible games, some already created and ready to use.

Peer Tutoring Practice Activities. Peer tutoring is an instructional activity that provides students a structured situation in which they work together, usually in pairs, to learn or practice a task. Peer tutoring is often associated with group or partner work; however, peer tutoring involves much more teacher-developed structure than just putting students into groups. Peer tutoring also includes several specific approaches such as cross-age tutoring; peer-assisted learning strategies in reading and math, sometimes referred to as PALS; and reciprocal peer tutoring. Although there are many different names for peer tutoring, there are a few core principles across the various approaches.

Even though peer tutoring can be used to practice a variety of math skills such as basic facts, computation, and problem solving, we are going to apply the general principles of peer tutoring to the practice of important math vocabulary. For our purposes, we will specifically discuss reciprocal peer tutoring activities occurring within a typical math class where each student has the opportunity to be a tutor and a tutee. Additionally, it is important to note that because we are focusing on *practice*, the implication is that students have already received initial instruction on the vocabulary terms and are now receiving additional opportunities to expand their knowledge of the terms and/or practice using the vocabulary during a peer tutoring activity.

Now we are ready to discuss the important components to consider when developing peer tutoring activities to help students practice using essential math vocabulary. According to the Access Center on Improving Outcomes for All Students K–8 (www.k8accesscenter .org), there are six general principles to consider when designing a peer tutoring practice activity:

1. The teacher trains students on the process of peer tutoring and strategies for fulfilling their role of tutor or tutee.

2. The teacher assigns partners.

3. Students retrieve their tutoring materials prepared by the teacher.

4. Students follow a highly structured tutoring procedure, in which tutors present material previously covered by the teacher, and provide feedback to the tutee.

5. Students switch roles after the teacher's signal. The tutee becomes the tutor.

6. The teacher circulates around the room, monitoring and providing feedback.

It is obvious that peer tutoring is a very structured instructional activity. We will now discuss each of the six steps.

Step 1: Because peer tutoring activities are very structured, teachers must teach the students their roles expected during the activity. Our peer tutoring activity will have a specific correction procedure; therefore, the teacher must take some time to teach students the correction procedure and confirm that all students are able to execute the correction procedure accurately. Do not underestimate students' ability to learn and correctly apply the correction procedures. Actually, once students have learned the correction procedure, students are quick to correct their teacher; after all, students really enjoy playing the role of the teacher. Depending on the students' ages and abilities, plan to spend 10 minutes across three to four days to train students in the expected procedures for peer tutoring.

Step 2: Assigning students to their partner is also a very important step, obviously. Among other things, consider social issues within your class as well as ability levels of your students. One common approach in peer tutoring for assigning partners is to rank students' achievement from highest to lowest. Then, divide the list into a top half and a bottom half. Next, match students following this pattern: The highest student in the top half is assigned to the highest student in the bottom half, the next highest student in the top half is assigned to next highest student in the bottom half, and so on until all students are assigned. This method avoids always pairing the highest student with the lowest student—not a good practice. Remember, there is no absolute rule for the assigning of partners, and teacher judgment is always important.

Step 3: Since peer tutoring activities usually require students to access materials organized in folders, it is important to make sure students know the process of accessing materials. Another reason for training students in accessing materials is to reduce the time it takes to get materials so instructional time can maximized. Of course, the teacher can always be in charge of passing out the materials, but that might actually take longer than having students get their materials. It is best to have a very organized system in place where materials are stored in one location and students know exactly how they are expected to get their materials.

Step 4: Because it is essential that all students are indeed engaging with the targeted vocabulary, it is important to have structured materials already developed for the students to use during the peer tutoring activity. Generally, teachers develop cards or sheets to guide the students through the activities and prompt the tutor when a correction is needed. Try to keep the procedures as simple and explicit as possible to reduce students' tendency to go off task.

Let's take a closer look at a peer tutoring sequence for the terms *acute angle* and *variable* using the Frayer Model as the main instructional anchor. Since peer tutoring is best used after students have learned the new vocabulary word, Figure 9.2 is anchored with the Frayer Model used to teach students the term *acute angle*.

Figure 9.2   Example Peer Tutoring Instructional Activity Using the Frayer Model.

Tutor: The purpose of this lesson is to remember and understand the important math vocabulary terms that we have been learning over the past week during math class. (Tutor states the learning objective.) You will practice telling me what a term means when I show it to you and then give me one to two important facts or characteristics about the term, and then provide an example and a nonexample. If you get stuck, I will help you.

Tutor is looking at a Frayer Model for the term acute angle. Tutee cannot see the Frayer Model:

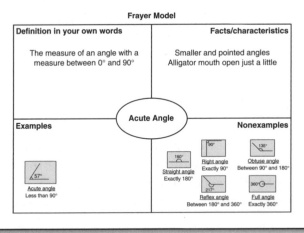

Tutor: Look at this term, acute angle. Tell me what it means.

Tutee: An angle between 0 and 90 degrees. It is small. (If no response, tutor provides definition.)

Tutor: Good! An acute angle is an angle that measures between 0 and 90 degrees. Now, tell me one more time what an acute angle means.

Tutor: Excellent. Now, can you tell me a fact or characteristics about an acute angle?

Tutee: It is a small angle.

Tutor: Great! Anything else? (If not, move to next question.)

Tutor: Now I want you to give me an example of an acute angle. You can either draw it with your pencil or point to an example in the room. What is your example?

Tutee: I will draw my example for you.

Tutor: That is correct! The example you drew me looks like an acute angle because it is between 0 and 90 degrees.

Tutor: Now I want you to give me a nonexample of an acute angle. You can either draw it with your pencil or point to a nonexample in the room. What is your nonexample?

Tutor: That is correct! The nonexample you drew me doesn't look like an acute angle because it is bigger than 90 degrees.

Tutor: Great work! An acute angle is an angle that measures between 0 and 90 degrees. (Go on to the next word or switch roles.)

Source: Adapted from www.k8accesscenter.org/training_resources/mathpeer tutoring.asp

Keep in mind there is no one way or right way to set up a peer tutoring activity, but rather certain aspects should be considered to maximize the students' on-task time. This is best achieved with specific and explicit procedures in place for the students to follow. In the Figure 9.2 example, directions to the students are very clear in what the tutor is to ask, materials are also very structured, and a correction procedure is outlined for the students.

Step 5: In our peer tutoring activities, we are focusing on reciprocal peer tutoring where each student gets a chance to be the tutor and the tutee. These roles can also be called coach and player. The point here is to make sure each student has an opportunity to lead his or her partner. Although not necessary, it is recommended that teachers set up specific time allocations for peer tutoring activities. In the example with index cards, each student has 90 seconds to practice, and then roles are switched. By adding a time component, teachers can keep things moving more efficiently because everyone knows there is only so much time. This also helps keep the teacher on target regarding instructional time. It is best to provide students multiple smaller practice sessions distributed across several days rather than a few 60-minute practice sessions. Timing allotments of 10 minutes are recommended for peer tutoring activities focusing on math vocabulary.

Step 6: The teacher should be circulating around the room while students are practicing with their partners. This serves at least two purposes. First, teachers can monitor students for executing correct procedures, especially the correction procedure. In math, it is important to reduce the number of times a student practices something incorrectly because the error can become learned by the student. That is, if a student practices a vocabulary word incorrectly enough times, the student can actually learn the term incorrectly. In this situation, it may take much longer to undo the student's learned error. Ensure partners are executing the correction procedures correctly every time. Second, this is a great opportunity to provide positive reinforcement to students who are working well with their partner.

Clearly, there is flexibility within the six components previously discussed depending on students' ages and abilities as well as the math vocabulary being targeted. The important aspect of this activity is to provide a structured peer tutoring activity for *all* students to have multiple opportunities to practice using essential math vocabulary. Also, the addition of a specific correction procedure is essential to preventing the learning of incorrect meanings.

In summary, the Access Center (n.d.) outlines six tips for successfully implementing peer tutoring activities: (1) design lessons to reinforce skills already taught to students, (2) identify specific learning objectives to be presented by the tutor, (3) teach students how to be tutors, (4) provide a script or prompts for the tutor, (5) provide necessary flash cards or a list of skills to the tutor, and (6) provide a daily log to record tutoring sessions.

Academic Vocabulary Notebook. Beyond the initial instruction, an important step of effective vocabulary instruction is helping students keep an accurate and comprehensive record of the words that they have been taught and learned (Marzano, 2004). This can be accomplished by using a structured academic vocabulary notebook or a derivative of student journals focused on vocabulary. Remember that students are introduced very quickly to a large volume of math-specific terms, and it is foolish to expect students to commit all of these terms and definitions to long-term memory without some type of organized system that can be revisited frequently throughout the course of the school year.

Young children will need help organizing and keeping their vocabulary notebook. This notebook could be organized in a variety of ways such as three-ringed binders, regular composition notebooks, and other age-appropriate systems that teachers have created. Three-ringed binders, for example, can be easily expanded and are able to hold plastic pockets where index cards can be stored. The best advice for developing an academic vocabulary notebook is to keep it simple. Creating a very complex and complicated system may actually discourage students more than encourage them.

Technology may offer more efficient and effective ways to keep academic vocabulary notebooks. For example, take a moment to explore the following link from the Oklahoma State Department of Education: http://ok.gov/sde/sites/ok.gov.sde/files/BAVSample .pdf. This document includes several useful resources for keeping a vocabulary notebook. Figures 9.3, 9.4, and 9.5 are a few screen captures from the document.

As mathematical vocabulary continues to emerge as an essential instructional and learning goal, more resources specific to math vocabulary will become available from state departments of education, mostly likely at no cost to educators, such as the example from Oklahoma.

Conclusion

There is no question as to the importance of students learning to use the language of mathematics; however, the importance of spending instructional time specifically to teach math vocabulary is still underrecognized. For students to become actively engaged in mathematics past the mundane computational requirements, vocabulary development is essential.

Figure 9.3   Vocabulary Worksheet From the Oklahoma State
Department of Education

Vocabulary Worksheet

Term: _____ My Understanding: 1   2   3   4

Describe: _____

_____

_____

_____

Draw: | Activity:

Subject:

Term: _____ My Understanding: 1   2   3   4

Describe: _____

_____

_____

_____

Draw: | Activity:

Page 4 of 12

Source: http://ok.gov/sde/sites/ok.gov.sde/files/BAVSample.pdf

Figure 9.4   Vocabulary Model From the Oklahoma State Department of Education

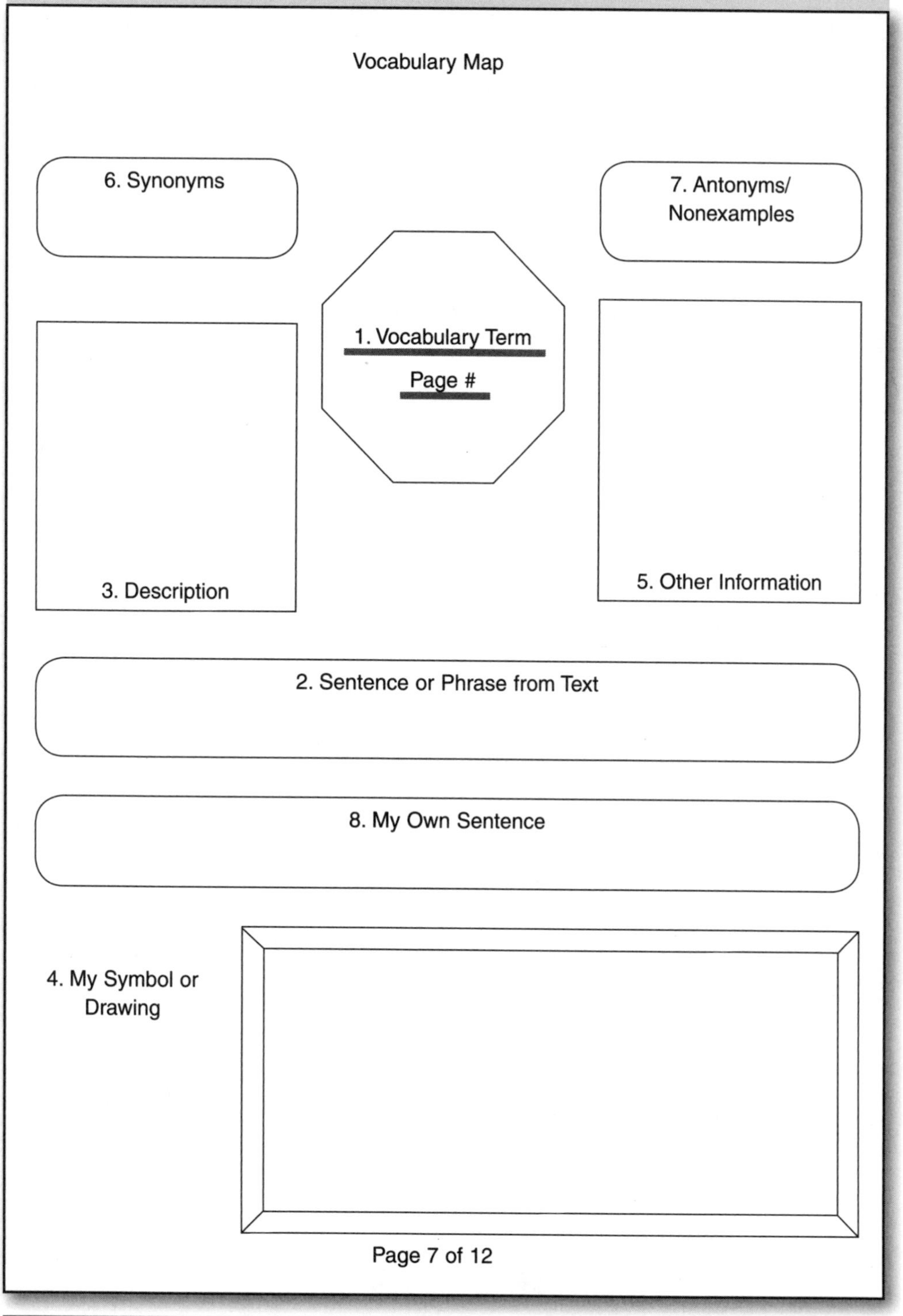

Vocabulary Map

6. Synonyms

7. Antonyms/ Nonexamples

1. Vocabulary Term

Page #

3. Description

5. Other Information

2. Sentence or Phrase from Text

8. My Own Sentence

4. My Symbol or Drawing

Page 7 of 12

Source: http://ok.gov/sde/sites/ok.gov.sde/files/BAVSample.pdf

Figure 9.5   Vocabulary Progress Chart From the Oklahoma State
Department of Education

Vocabulary Progress Chart

✓+	I understand even more about the term than I have been taught.
✓	I understand the term and am not confused about its meaning or usage.
✓−	I am not sure I understand the term, but I have some idea as to its meaning.
×	I really do not understand the term at all.

Progress Chart	Color the box to show your level of knowledge about each term			
Write each term below.	✓+	✓	✓−	×

Page 11 of 12

Source: http://ok.gov/sde/sites/ok.gov.sde/files/BAVSample.pdf

References

Access Center: Improving Outcomes for All Students K–8. (n.d.). *Using peer tutoring for math.* Retrieved October 17, 2011, from www.k8accesscenter .org/training_resources/mathpeertutoring.asp

Adams, T. L. (2003). Reading mathematics: More than words can say. *The Reading Teacher, 56*(8), 786–795.

Biemiller, A. (2004). Teaching vocabulary in the primary grades: Vocabulary instruction is needed. In J. F. Baumann & E. J. Kame'enui (Eds.), *Vocabulary instruction: Research to practice.* New York: Guilford Press.

Common Core State Standards for Mathematics. (n.d.). Retrieved June 1, 2011, from the Council of Chief State School Officers and the National Governors Association website: http://corestandards.org/assets/ CCSSI_Math%20Standards.pdf

Garrett, S. (n.d.). *Vocabulary notebook sample packet.* Available from the State Superintendent of Public Instruction, Oklahoma State Department of Education. Retrieved October 15, 2010, from http://ok.gov/sde/sites/ ok.gov.sde/files/BAVSample.pdf

Hart, B. & Risley, T. (1995). *Meaningful differences in the everyday experience of young American children.* Baltimore: Paul H. Brookes.

Kilpatrick, J., Swafford, J., & Findell, B. (Eds.). (2001). *Adding it up: Helping children learn mathematics.* Washington, DC: National Research Council.

Marzano, R. J. (2004). *Building background knowledge for academic achievement.* Alexandria, VA: Association for Supervision and Curriculum Development.

Mastropieri, M. A., & Scruggs, T. E. (2010). *The inclusive classroom: Strategies for effective instruction* (4th ed.). Upper Saddle River, NJ: Prentice Hall.

National Council of Teachers of Mathematics. (1989). *Curriculum and evaluation standards for school mathematics.* Reston, VA: Author.

National Council of Teachers of Mathematics. (2000). *Principles and standards for school mathematics.* Reston, VA: Author.

Riccomini, P. J., Sanders, S., & Jones, J. (2008). The key to enhancing students' mathematical vocabulary knowledge. *Journal on School Educational Technology, 4*(1), 1–7.

Riccomini, P. J., & Witzel, B. S. (2010). *Response to intervention in mathematics.* Thousand Oaks, CA: Corwin.

Rubenstein, R., & Thompson, D. (2002). Understanding and supporting children's mathematical vocabulary development. *Teaching Children Mathematics, 9*(2), 107–112.

10

The Next Steps to Teaching Number Sense

The K–5 standards provide students with a *solid foundation in whole numbers, addition, subtraction, multiplication, division, fractions and decimals*—which help young students build the foundation to successfully apply more demanding math concepts and procedures, and move into applications.

Common Core State Standards in Mathematics, http://www .corestandards.org/assets/KeyPointsMath.pdf

Planning

Understanding number sense sets the foundation in mathematics. Students relate best to practices in which they can apply their knowledge of number sense through given activities. When you begin planning lessons and activities, implement real-life scenarios and hands-on experiences as often as possible. Planning should take place in a variety of settings. Educators should work together as a grade level as well as in vertically aligned grade-level teams.

Horizontal (Grade-Level) Alignment

When planning as a grade level, all student abilities are considered. Objectives should be the first discussion in a planning meeting. Objectives are found by looking through the Common Core State Standards (CCSS). Once the objective is decided upon, assessments should be designed to meet that objective. Assessments are often thought of as an end goal; however, assessments should be used as a vehicle for improvement, not just pass or fail. A timetable should be set for the objectives to be mastered. Finally, begin sifting through resources and have a collaborative discussion with your colleagues to plan lessons and activities that are highly engaging and rigorous for student learning. In the grade level, you must look at three levels of student achievement. Your students will most likely perform in a low, middle, and high group, needing remediation, support, or acceleration on a specific skill. Keep in mind that students in a remediation group will need extra support and scaffolding to meet the desired objective, while those in an accelerating group will need to be challenged further. Effective planning always keeps the levels of learners in mind so the proper assistance can be provided during each lesson. Keep at hand an outline of what is needed for a strong lesson, and use it to go by while planning your lesson and discussing it with colleagues. An example is provided in Figure 10.1.

Figure 10.1   Outline for Planning a Lesson

1. Determine the objective.

2. What prior knowledge is needed to meet this objective? Provide background information if needed.

3. Choose a task, a lesson, or an activity.

4. Provide possible strategies and resources.

5. Plan a mini-lesson. What do you think the students will do, and how will you question and assist during the lesson?

6. Reflection. All lessons need to end with a strong reflection—this sums up your objective for the lesson that day. Don't run out of time for a reflection; always make the time.

Grade-level planning and assessments are crucial to monitor the growth and achievement of students. However, vertical planning is just as important to keep students from having gaps in learning and to find ways to close the gaps that are preexisting.

Horizontal planning does not have to be restricted to mathematics instruction. Horizontal planning can exist across content and standards to better show contextual use of mathematics as well as other content areas.

Literacy

Precedence exists to integrate literacy with mathematics. Three areas of literacy to be discussed are communication, reading, and writing. Through the connection of literacy and the CCSS, teachers can integrate literature into math, science, and social studies.

Children's literature has always been a love in education among students and teachers. Often literature can be used to introduce and/or support a skill, and even be applied to a closure of a unit of study on specific skills. Engagement through literature allows students the ability to recall facts from the story that relate to math applications. Several series are written to assist in student learning in mathematics through children's literature (see Table 10.1). A *Math Adventure* series falls in an upper-elementary category, while author Stuart J. Murphy has several books for primary grades.

Table 10.1   Children's Literature Series for Mathematics Understanding

Book Title	Skill	Common Core State Standards
A Place for Zero: A Math Adventure by Angeline Sparagna Lopresti *Sir Cumference and All the Kings Tens: A Math Adventure* by Cindy Neuschwander	place value, standard form, expanded form	2.NBT.3. Read and write numbers to 1,000 using base-ten numerals, number names, and expanded form.
The Very Hungry Caterpillar by Eric Carle	counting	K.CC.4. Understand the relationship between numbers and quantities; connect counting to cardinality.
More or Less by Stuart J. Murphy	comparing numbers, counting	K.CC.6. Identify whether the number of objects in one group is greater than, less than, or equal to the number of objects in another group, e.g., by using matching and counting strategies.

(Continued)

Table 10.1 (Continued)

Book Title	Skill	Common Core State Standards
Two of Everything by Lily Toy Hong	addition, multiples	2.NBT.2. Count within 1,000; skip-count by 5s, 10s, and 100s.
Elevator Magic by Stuart J. Murphy	subtraction, decreasing numbers	1.OA.1. Use addition and subtraction within 20 to solve word problems involving situations of adding to, taking from, putting together, taking apart, and comparing, with unknowns in all positions, e.g., by using objects, drawings, and equations with a symbol for the unknown number to represent the problem.
Safari Park by Stuart J. Murphy	missing addends/ subtrahends	1.OA.4. Understand subtraction as an unknown-addend problem. *For example, subtract 10 – 8 by finding the number that makes 10 when added to 8.*
Amanda Bean's Amazing Dream by Cindy Neuschwander *One Hundred Hungry Ants* by Elinor J. Pinczes	multiplication, arrays	2.OA.4. Use addition to find the total number of objects arranged in rectangular arrays with up to 5 rows and up to 5 columns; write an equation to express the total as a sum of equal addends.
The Doorbell Rang by Pat Hutchins *A Remainder of One* by Elinor J. Pinczes	division	3.OA.7. Fluently multiply and divide within 100, using strategies such as the relationship between multiplication and division (e.g., knowing that $8 \times 5 = 40$, one knows $40 \div 5 = 8$) or properties of operations. By the end of Grade 3, know from memory all products of two one-digit numbers.
Changes, Changes by Pat Hutchins *The Greedy Triangle* by Marilyn Burns *If You Were a Polygon* by Marcie Aboff	geometric shapes	1.G.2. Compose two-dimensional shapes (rectangles, squares, trapezoids, triangles, half-circles, and quarter-circles) or three-dimensional shapes (cubes, right rectangular prisms, right circular cones, and right circular cylinders) to create a composite shape, and compose new shapes from the composite shape. 1.G.1. Distinguish between defining attributes (e.g., triangles are closed and three-sided) versus non-defining attributes (e.g., color, orientation, overall size); build and draw shapes to possess defining attributes.

Book Title	Skill	Common Core State Standards
		K.G.4. Analyze and compare two- and three-dimensional shapes, in different sizes and orientations, using informal language to describe their similarities, differences, parts (e.g., number of sides and vertices/"corners"), and other attributes (e.g., having sides of equal length).
Inch by Inch by Leo Lionni *How Big Is a Foot?* by Rolf Myller *Measuring Penny* by Loreen Leedy *Math Counts* series by Henry Plukrose *Equal Shmequal* by Virginia L. Kroll	measurement	1.MD.1. Order three objects by length; compare the lengths of two objects indirectly by using a third object. 1.MD.2. Express the length of an object as a whole number of length units, by laying multiple copies of a shorter object (the length unit) end to end; understand that the length measurement of an object is the number of same-size length units that span it with no gaps or overlaps. *Limit to contexts where the object being measured is spanned by a whole number of length units with no gaps or overlaps.*
Full House: An Invitation to Fractions by Dayle Ann Dodds *Piece = Part = Portion* by Scott Gifford *The Hershey's Milk Chocolate Bar Fractions Book* by Jerry Pallotta *Give Me Half!* by Stuart J. Murphy	fractions	3.NF.1. Understand a fraction $1/b$ as the quantity formed by 1 part when a whole is partitioned into b equal parts; understand a fraction a/b as the quantity formed by a parts of size $1/b$.
Benny's Pennies by Pat Brisson *The Penny Pot* by Stuart J. Murphy *Once Upon a Dime: A Math Adventure* by Nancy Kelly Allen	money	2.MD.8. Solve word problems involving dollar bills, quarters, dimes, nickels, and pennies, using $ and ¢ symbols appropriately. *Example: If you have 2 dimes and 3 pennies, how many cents do you have?*

(Continued)

Table 10.1   (Continued)

Book Title	Skill	Common Core State Standards
Midnight Fright by Kathryn Heling *The Grouchy Ladybug* by Eric Carle *The Clock Struck One: A Time-Telling Tale* by Trudy Harris	time	1.MD.3. Tell and write time in hours and half-hours using analog and digital clocks. 1.MD3. Tell and write time in hours and half-hours using analog and digital clocks.
Lemonade for Sale by Stuart J. Murphy *The Best Vacation Ever* by Stuart J. Murphy *Tally O'Malley* by Stuart J. Murphy	data analysis	1.MD.4. Organize, represent, and interpret data with up to three categories; ask and answer questions about the total number of data points, how many in each category, and how many more or less are in one category than in another.

Develop lessons around the themes in the literature books to better show the relevance of the mathematics through the social context of each story.

Writing

An easy way to integrate writing and mathematics is to have students create math content stories. Using children's literature about math skills opens the doors for students to think creatively and make their own stories. Writing a short story, length depending on age of student, can be an easy assessment to check on students' writing and their understanding of the math concept through application. An example would be to have students write a story about time, modeling a story like *The Grouchy Ladybug*. They can stamp the page with an analog clock stamp; fill in the time based on hour, half-hour, quarter-hour, and five- or one-minute intervals; and create something that happens at each time. This could be used for elapsed time in the upper grades.

Social Studies and Science

Two areas in early childhood that the CCSS do not specifically address are social studies and science. However, math and literacy components of the CCSS can easily integrate into social studies and science. Those familiar with the CCSS in language arts know of the increased emphasis on content area literacy early in a child's schooling. Both social studies and science are ideal content areas for applying nonfiction text to mathematics. Our economic system can pull in money, data, time, counting principles, writing, reading, and so much more. Science experiments are math related in hypothesis and exploration. When reading through your state standards for social studies and science, consider all the other content areas that can be brought in to make the lesson and activity more rigorous and engaging to the students and learning.

A Second-Grade Classroom Economy

Objective: Students will be able to create, advertise, and sell a good for consumers (classmates and staff). Students will be able to make change for consumers and calculate the profits made after paying back the loan and taxes on their supplies. The class will graph the outcome of sales and reflect on supply and demand.

Lesson: Have students work in small groups of two to four to create a good. This does not mean students should use a good that is already made; rather they will make and give the teacher a list of supplies needed in order to make their good. Some ideas include bookmarks, tissue-roll pencil holders, paintings, popsicle picture frames, and so on. Provide a few days for goods to be made. Students will then create a poster to advertise their product. Finally the groups will set the price. The teacher will set a price limit—for second graders, possibly no more than $1. Hold a classroom market day where other teachers and staff members from the school are able to come in the classroom and purchase goods. Allow groups to have a "bank" in order to give change when needed. Provide staff members with pretend dollars so the students will need to make the proper amount of change. The classroom market can take place for approximately one hour. Upon closing of the classroom market, the teacher will have students work in their groups to count up the money earned. Groups will then be asked to pay back money that was borrowed to make change for the market, taxes, and supply costs. Then students will be asked to split the money equally amongst team members. The final piece is to create a class graph to see which product had the highest demand and which product brought in the most profit.

Within this lesson on economy students are practicing with money, making change, using addition and subtraction principles, graphing data, and interpreting data in math content. Literacy components are used to create a persuasive advertisement. Social studies components used are supply and demand, goods and services, economics, and taxes.

Summary

Integration is key in providing a rigorous and engaging learning environment for students. Although not all areas can be easily integrated, try not to teach everything in isolation. Useful and effective team planning and grade-level and vertical teams are the best support for many teachers. The most frequent complaint is not having enough time to get it all done or to talk with the team and share ideas. Make it a priority. As a team, you can better meet the needs of all students. Integrating content areas will allow more time to step in and remediate, support, or accelerate students where their needs lie.

Outside Resources

Educational organizations continue to work hard to help districts, schools, and teachers develop their planning for the CCSS. Table 10.2 is not all-inclusive but includes some excellent websites designed to help support teachers' implementation of the CCSS. Use these as resources to guide planning and implementation of practices. In some cases, the content in the CCSS is different from what is traditionally presented in a classroom. Thus, professional development should focus on content as much as it does instructional practices in mathematics.

Table 10.2 State Department Websites for CCSS Implementation Support

Website	Organization	Purpose
http://www.corestandards.org/	Common Core State Standards Initiative	Details the grade-level domains and clusters as well as the overall math practices
http://www.k-5mathteachingresources.com/	K–5 Math Teaching Resources	Lessons and activities are connected to the CCSS by grade and topic including connections to math literacy

Website	Organization	Purpose
http://commoncoretools.me/	Bill McCallum and colleagues	Discussions and links to math resources such as progressions and the Illustrative Mathematics Project
http://www.ixl.com/math/ standards/	IXL	CCSS math word problems set to grade-level cluster pieces
http://www.pta.org/4446.htm	National Parent Teachers Association	Provides suggestions as to how parents can support their children through the CCSS
http://www.smarterbalanced .org/	Smarter Balanced Assessment Consortium	Describes the organization's work on assessment and direction about the CCSS
http://www.parcconline.org/	Partnership for Assessment of Readiness for College and Careers	Describes the organization's implementation of assessment practice for the CCSS

Index

Absolute value, 85
Abstract stage in CRA sequence
  for addition and subtraction, 60 (box),
    82 (box), 83 (box), 86 (box),
    87 (box)
  for multiplication, 96, 97 (table)
  for place value, 82 (box), 83 (box),
    86 (box), 87 (box)
  See also CRA sequence
Academic vocabulary notebook, 150–151,
  152(figure)–154(figure). *See also*
  Student journal of definitions
Access Center, 146, 150
Accuracy
  in addition and subtraction, 61
  calculators for checking, 106
  in counting, 46
  importance of, 6 (textbox), 12
  in letter naming, 53 (box)
  of mathematical vocabulary, 60, 128,
    142, 150
  in multiplication, 104, 105, 106
  in place value, 72, 80, 81
  in problem solving, 128, 134
Achievement in mathematics
  active engagement as a key to, 95
  grade-level progression and, 15, 19
  levels of, and grade-level planning, 158
  predictors of, 109, 124
  turning around, 2–4
  See also Assessment; Proficiency in
    mathematics

Acute angle, in peer tutoring example,
  148 (figure), 149 (box)
Adaptive reasoning, and math
  language, 138–139
Addends, missing, 63–64, 113–114,
  160 (table)
Addition and subtraction, 57–66
  algebra and, 112–115
  apps for, 68 (table)
  associative property of addition,
    63, 104 (table), 112
  cardinality and, 55–56, 60
  CCSS for, 57, 58 (table), 59 (table), 60
  CCSS standard algorithm for, 19–20
  children's literature for, 160 (table)
  commutative property of addition,
    57, 62, 63, 104 (table), 112
  counting and, 46, 47, 49, 50, 60
  CRA sequence in, 60–62, 81–83
  decomposition for, 60–61
  division and, 65–66
  error analysis of, 38
  fractions in, 65
  by grade level, 13–15, 57, 58 (table),
    59 (table), 60–66
  interrelationship of, 62–63, 82, 89
  intervention for, 66
  manipulatives for, 60, 62
  measurement and, 65, 116–117
  memorization in, 57, 61, 62–65, 68, 73
  multiplication and, 65–66, 95, 100, 101
  number facts in, 57, 57 (box), 62, 65

CORWIN
A SAGE Company

The Corwin logo—a raven striding across an open book—represents the union of courage and learning. Corwin is committed to improving education for all learners by publishing books and other professional development resources for those serving the field of PreK–12 education. By providing practical, hands-on materials, Corwin continues to carry out the promise of its motto: "Helping Educators Do Their Work Better."